The Leadership We Need

The Leadership We Need

A New Mindset for a Brighter Future

Maria Brinck

An imprint of John Murray Press

1

A CIP catalogue record for this title is available from the British Library

Hardback ISBN 9781399823425
Trade Paperback ISBN 9781399823432
ebook ISBN 9781399823449

Typeset by KnowledgeWorks Global Ltd.

Printed and bound in Great Britain by Clays Ltd, Elcograf S.p.A.

John Murray Press policy is to use papers that are natural, renewable and recyclable products and made from wood grown in sustainable forests. The logging and manufacturing processes are expected to conform to the environmental regulations of the country of origin.

John Murray Press ·   John Murray Business
Carmelite House   123 S. Broad St., Ste 2750
50 Victoria Embankment   Philadelphia, PA 19109
London EC4Y 0DZ

https://johnmurraybusiness.com/

John Murray Press, part of Hodder & Stoughton Limited
An Hachette UK company

The authorised representative in the EEA is Hachette Ireland,
8 Castlecourt Centre, Dublin 15, D15 XTP3, Ireland (email: info@hbgi.ie)

To Life and its essential balance between masculine and feminine.

Contents

The Goal of This Book

This book aims to challenge our ingrained mindset around leadership to one that I believe will serve us better for what is ahead. Mindsets control emotions and thinking, which in turn control our behaviors. To be able to change the world, we need to start with ourselves. This book contains inquiries and assessments to explore yours. Knowing yourself will awaken you to the best leader you can be.

INTRODUCTION

"Interesting Times"

This is a book about the opportunities and consequences await-
ing humanity in the decades ahead. These years are poised to be
the most pivotal in human history, marking an inflection point
where our trajectory could drastically change for better or
worse—we face two divergent paths leading to either utopia or
extinction. It is evident that a new type of leadership is required
to realize our human potential. This leadership must understand that we are all in this together and that full representation of humanity in leadership roles is necessary. Moreover, it
must recognize that all the money and power in the world will
be meaningless if we continue on our current path.

People tend to believe they live in an age of unique consequence. In 1936, Sir Austen Chamberlain, the brother of
British politican Neville Chamberlain, wrote to an American
diplomat, "Many years ago, I learned from one of our diplomats in China that one of the principal Chinese curses heaped
upon an enemy is 'May you live in an interesting age.' Surely
no age has been more fraught with insecurity than our own
present time."[1] Little did he know, things were about to get
much more "interesting."

While future generations may look back and recognize that
things haven't begun to get "interesting" for humanity, I wrote
this book because I believe we are living through a pivotal
and unparalleled period. I am reminded of Charles Dickens'

famous opening line from *A Tale of Two Cities*: "It was the best of times, it was the worst of times, it was the age of wisdom, it was the age of foolishness, it was the epoch of belief, it was the epoch of incredulity, it was the season of light, it was the season of darkness, it was the spring of hope, it was the winter of despair."[2]

We do, after all, live in the best of times. As former World Bank Group President Jim Yong Kim observed, "Over the last 25 years, more than a billion people have lifted themselves out of extreme poverty, and the global poverty rate is now lower than it has ever been in recorded history."[3] Since the start of the twenty-first century, battle deaths have dropped to close to zero per 100,000 people (the wars in Ukraine and Gaza have, of course, caused battle deaths to rise significantly, but the larger trend remains).[4] In primitive societies, 15 percent of people died violently—now it is 0.03 percent, meaning that the world today is about 500 times more peaceful than the one our ancestors inhabited.[5] We see similar progress in education, women's rights, democratic governance, and virtually every other metric humans have come up with to measure progress. A whole cottage industry has formed of people telling us how good we have it. These "prophets of positivity" include Steven Pinker and his excellent book *The Better Angels of Our Nature*,[6] Hans Rosling with *Factfulness: Ten Reasons We're Wrong About the World—And Why Things Are Better Than You Think*,[7] and Charles Kenny with *Getting Better: Why Global Development Is Succeeding—And How We Can Improve the World Even More*.[8]

For many people, the notion that we are living in a time of unparalleled peace and prosperity seems like a cruel joke. The wars in Ukraine, Yemen, and, more recently, the Gaza Strip paint a starkly different picture. Take a walk along the streets of San Francisco—home to the highest number of billionaires per capita of any city in the world—where areas now resemble refugee camps. A majority of adults in the USA (57 percent) believe that those aged 65 and older will have a worse standard of living in 2050 than they do today.[9] Given the looming environmental crisis, rampant inequality, internet-induced social isolation, falling living standards, declining mental health, and a host of other challenges, it's understandable why some might look back at past eras with envy, despite assurances from data that we've never had it better.

Will "the best of times" or "the worst of times" be a fitting description for the second half of the twenty-first century? Will it be a "season of light, a season of darkness, a spring of hope, a winter of despair"? Humanity has achieved a great deal in a relatively short time, but we are also just beginning. Considering that invertebrate species tend to exist for roughly 11 million years, and humans have been around for about 200,000 years, if we compare that 11 million years to a 73-year lifespan (the life expectancy as of 2022), then we are akin to 18-month-old infants. Reflect on all the beauty and wonder we have created, and how much more we have yet to discover and unleash.

In 2001, Ray Kurzweil, Google's head of engineering, published a seminal essay titled "The Law of Accelerating Returns." In it, he notes, "Our ancestors expected the future to be pretty much like their present, which had been pretty much like their past. We expect the changes over the next 100 years to mirror the changes of the last 100 years. But in the 21st century, we might see the equivalent of 20,000 years of progress (at today's rate)."[10]

Blogger Tim Urban uses vivid imagery to underscore precisely what this means (see Figure 0.1).[11] This is where we currently stand. Somewhere along the line in Figure 0.1, we learned to tame fire, followed by electricity. Copernicus discovered that the Earth wasn't at the center of the universe and Einstein realized that time was relative. If the line stretches

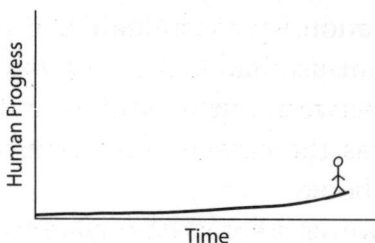

Figure 0.1 Where we stand now (*Source*: Tim Urban)

18 months, we invented the wheel 17 days ago, the printing press 36 hours ago, and the internet 10 seconds ago. Can you imagine what tomorrow will bring? Probably not, because if Kurzweil is correct, human progress will look like Figure 0.2 in the next few hours of our 73-year life.

The possibilities are terrifying, wonderful, and infinite. If we manage to make it to our second birthday, we will likely by then have figured out how to extend our life expectancy as a species past 11 million years, outliving even crocodiles, which have been around for 85 million years.

Of course, there is one big caveat. Because of our progress, the chances of making it to tomorrow are much worse than most people realize, as Chapter 1 explores. The philosopher Toby Ord captures our current predicament beautifully in his observation, "As the gap between our power and our wisdom grows, our future is subject to an ever-increasing level

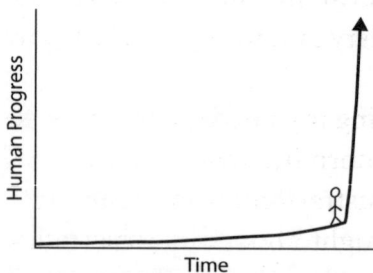

Figure 0.2 Where we are headed (*Source*: Tim Urban)

of risk. This situation is unsustainable."[12] It was the realization of just how unsustainable the situation is today, with the lack of balance between our masculine and feminine human qualities, that was the catalyst for getting words on paper and writing this book.

There was, however, a second motivation. I wish I could say that it came from a grand revelation, something selfless and noble. But it was actually a simple family dispute that started in May of 2021. My mother's uncle, Anders, had entrusted his estate to my mother's brother, my uncle. Anders had assumed that it would be shared evenly between the two siblings. After Anders passed, however, my uncle informed my mother that the estate would, in fact, not be shared. The family home was the place of her childhood memories. Anders' home on Lake Vänern, the largest in Sweden, was a happy place where she felt at peace. And now she was being told that nothing was going to be shared with her. My uncle is not necessarily a bad person, but like many of us, he measures his self-worth by possessions—and possessions he has: a collection of Porsches, a collection of Rolexes, and now the estate. My mother, a widow of 10 years and his only sibling, was being left out in the cold. To top it off, my mother had been the caretaker of Anders' wife Ingrid, wheelchair-bound for more than 10 years following a stroke. As has happened throughout our history and continues to this day, the woman does all the caregiving in the family while the man gets all the financial rewards. And money equals power in our society and the cycle of patriarchal power continues. I was angry.

After confronting my uncle, sure that this was a mistake or a bad joke, and confirming that he simply didn't want to share, I took out my frustration on my journal, furiously scribbling down what I thought about this situation. I wrote how it was the twenty-first century yet we are still continuously dealing with unequal power distributions, where men take what they want, and the pain this inflicts on everyone else.

This book will touch on the controversial subject of innate gender differences between men and women. Masculinity, like femininity, is a complex and culturally influenced concept that can vary widely from one society to another over time. It's important, for both ethical and advantageous reasons, to evaluate people as individuals rather than based on their gender. Yet it is clear that there are traits and instincts that men are more likely to demonstrate. Some of these are positive: protectiveness, strength, resilience, courage, adventurousness. My uncle, however, was showing the worst: dominance and callousness in the pursuit of money, power, and status.

I blamed these masculine instincts for my uncle's actions. I wrote about how dangerous they are and about the coming catastrophes that await us unless we change, embracing the equally important feminine qualities of inclusion, compassion, and caring for others. I kept writing. Then I began researching. I wrote some more and researched some more. After several hours I had forgotten about my uncle (well, almost) as I ventured down the rabbit hole where I would remain for the next two years. When I finally emerged, I had written the book you are reading now. Unfortunately, my family still has a lot of healing to do and time has run out for my uncle to do right by his sister. My beloved mother Anna passed away from cancer in June, 2023.

Though this family dispute was the catalyst for getting words down on paper, in hindsight this book truly began 14 years ago when Earth's destruction suddenly became real to me.

It was 2008, and I needed a break from corporate America. I wanted to add some greater purpose to my life, something meaningful, something that would make the world a better place. Unfortunately, this is difficult to find within the confines of corporate environments, where the bottom line and shareholder profits often overshadow broader societal or environmental concerns. After spending four years immersed in the competitive ethos of an American business school, followed by eight years navigating the corporate landscape, I felt an overwhelming urge to broaden my horizons. I realized that my perspectives, values, and behaviors were heavily influenced by an American-centric worldview, and I began to question its adequacy in aligning with my fundamental values and overall sense of well-being.

Compelled by this realization, I embarked on a six-month journey away from the United States and into the heart of southern Cameroon. There, nestled within the lush expanse of the Congo Basin Rainforest, I volunteered at a chimpanzee and gorilla rescue centre. This experience not only marked a pivotal chapter in my life but also laid the groundwork for the reflections and insights that would eventually culminate in this book.

My journey led me to the quaint villages surrounding Belabo, a tranquil town nestled about an hour from our camp. Here, I witnessed a distinctive form of leadership. Tribal chiefs, embodying calm and patience, would sit in circles with community members, adopting a listening-first approach. They spoke only after everyone else had their say, ensuring every voice was heard and valued. This approach struck me as profoundly impactful, prompting me to ponder how transformative it could be if applied back home, promising significant benefits.

Yet this leadership style is a rarity in leadership meetings where leaders are expected to be the loudest, most dominant person in the room, whose wisdom is not to be questioned.

Intriguingly, these tribal leaders also demonstrated a balanced consideration of both long-term impacts and immediate outcomes in their decision-making processes. This was vividly illustrated in their thoughtful approach to something as simple as cutting down a tree, a stark departure from the short-term profit focus prevalent in the corporate world in which leaders prioritize immediate gains to satisfy investors, neglecting the long-term repercussions. (As Microsoft executive Sam Schillace put it, it would be an "absolutely fatal error at this moment to worry about things that can be fixed later.")[13]

My time among the indigenous communities of the Congo Basin Rainforest unveiled another profound insight: a deep-rooted connection with and respect for the natural world. This bond wasn't limited to human relationships but extended to the land, the flora, and the fauna, embodying a sense of "oneness." This profound connection imbued the villagers' lives with meaning and a sense of belonging—a sentiment I felt was largely absent in Western societies. Unique, invaluable knowledge and practices in environmental sustainability are taught by one generation to the next, and instead of conquering nature we live alongside nature in a symbiotic relationship.

Observing the local knowledge in these communities, I saw the value they placed on seeing nature and all living beings as part of an extended family. This perspective fostered a nurturing attitude toward life, offering them a purpose that seemed to elude many in the West. While it wouldn't be accurate to claim that all indigenous people are content, their lives are undoubtedly enriched with meaning and interconnectedness. They prioritize collaboration and cooperation, embodying the proverb, "It takes a village to raise a child." Feminine values are strong, in stark contrast to the competitive, individualistic masculine lifestyle prevalent in America where supposedly you are "self-made."

The indigenous communities' overarching sense of purpose starkly contrasts with the Western pursuit of keeping up with the Joneses, driven by material success and a competitive ethos. This difference in values highlights a profound disconnect in Western societies, where an emphasis on "self," material success, and a type-A leadership style has left many feeling isolated and unfulfilled. It's a concerning trend, especially given the higher prevalence of psychopathic traits among business executives compared with the general population, indicating a lack of empathy and compassion.

If we turn our gaze specifically toward the domain of leadership, it becomes clear that a significant majority of the leadership models prevalent in today's corporate world—69, to be precise—were conceived within a framework that not only prioritizes masculine perspectives but also aligns predominantly with Western ideology.[14] We have not yet even scratched the surface of human leadership potential, instead an unconscious bias has shaped our perception of "who" is qualified and capable to lead, setting business, nations and humanity back in unimaginable ways. This reality led me to ponder deeply on how such a narrow foundation has molded our collective understanding of what it means to lead, and to question the efficacy and inclusivity of these prevailing models. In this book, I advocate for a paradigm shift in leadership— a shift that necessitates the blending of both feminine and masculine energies, advocating for a leadership style that is not only balanced but also profoundly holistic. It is imperative that we extend our horizons to embrace and incorporate the rich tapestry of leadership wisdom that flourishes within non-Western cultures. The need of the hour is to transcend the myopic, profit-centric leadership models that dominate our current business landscape in favor of a perspective that is truly global and inclusive, one that values collective well-being over individual gain.

This urgent call for a broader perspective is echoed in our collective responsibility toward Indigenous peoples, who, while constituting less than 5 percent of the global population, are the custodians of over 80 percent of the world's biodiversity. Their dedication to preserving our planet's ecological diversity, often at significant personal risk, starkly contrasts with the extractive practices of fossil fuel, mining, and logging enterprises, such as those we encountered near our camp in Belabo. This glaring disparity not only highlights the critical need for a global reassessment of our values and priorities but also underscores the indispensable role that indigenous communities play in the stewardship of our planet's health. Recognizing and protecting the rights and wisdom of these communities is not just a moral imperative but a crucial step toward ensuring the sustainability and well-being of our global ecosystem.

Cameroon is situated in the Congo Basin Rainforest, the world's second-largest rainforest and carbon reservoir. It's quite beautiful and known for its rich biodiversity, which includes more than 200 mammal species, 300 reptiles, and 600 birds in addition to 9,000 species of plants.[15] Watching this beauty and diversity disappear before my eyes added meaning to the statistics and was an experience I won't soon forget.

Unfortunately, Cameroon has been one of the countries hardest hit by the twin ravages of deforestation and climate change. Like many other parts of the world, including my current home of Colorado, fires are growing out of control. From 2001 to 2023, Cameroon experienced a loss of 7,510 hectares of tree cover due to fires and 2,040,000 hectares from other causes of deforestation, around the size of San Francisco and New Jersey, respectively.[16] As a result, Cameroon's wildlife is disappearing, and its people are struggling to survive. Its rainforests are home to some of the world's most endangered animals, including gorillas, chimpanzees, and forest elephants already threatened by poaching and the destruction of their habitat by slash-and-burn agriculture. Its rivers are being polluted by mining companies, killing the fish that people have relied on as their primary source of protein for centuries.

While there, I learned about the experience of a man named Rodrigue Ngonzo. Rodrigue was born in Belabo and eventually went on to become board president of a group called Forêts et Développement Rural, which advocates for the sustainable use of Cameroon's natural resources. "The forest disappeared around the town. The climate became hotter. The rhythms of the rains changed," observed Rodrigue. "In the past, we would catch animals in front of our house, because we were so close to the forest. We used to play with pangolins when I was young—now a protected species in Cameroon—as we found them easily. Not anymore."[17]

While at the rescue center in Cameroon, I met Arvid, a one-year-old orphaned chimpanzee. He was the mischief of them all and yet a very sensitive little guy. He didn't like me at first and bit me more than once, but when he finally took a liking to me it was profound. Unfortunately, a few years after leaving the rescue center I got word that Arvid had contracted meningitis and passed away. Arvid's profound love and spirit will always be with me, and his voice can be heard throughout this book.

Following Cameroon, I began to think about how failures in leadership and the actions of highly compensated officials and

Figure 0.3 Arvid and I, connecting in Congo Basin Rainforest, Cameroon

business executives worldwide are contributing to our ongoing ecological crisis. This realization was the catalyst for founding Zynergy International in 2013, a leadership advisory firm dedicated to addressing these critical issues. In today's world, the influence of corporations has eclipsed that of nations, with 69 of the world's 100 largest economies being corporations.[18] Moreover, the once-clear demarcation between business executives and government officials is increasingly blurred, as multinational corporations wield their formidable power and control over media, finance, and agriculture. This influence allows them to intervene in, and even obstruct, international treaty negotiations to safeguard their business interests, often at a considerable cost to the environment and, most notably, to indigenous populations.

The urgency of rectifying leadership in business and extricating monetary influence from politics and international treaty negotiations cannot be overstated. Our collective survival hinges on this pivotal shift. A glaring testament to the current system's failure was the 29th unsuccessful United Nations Conference of the Parties (UN COP), held in Baku, Azerbaijan, in November 2024, after which, despite numerous meetings, carbon dioxide emissions continue to rise unabated. This trend underscores the critical need for a new direction in how we approach leadership and governance, one that prioritizes the health of our planet and the well-being of all its inhabitants over the narrow interests of the few. The time for transformative change is now, and it begins with reimagining leadership for a sustainable future.

Every year air pollution alone kills nine million people, just one of the many atrocious statistics indicative of a leadership crisis.[19] We witnessed the failure in the response to Covid-19, which has now claimed more than seven million lives.[20] These deaths weren't inevitable but rather examples of choices made by businesses and governments. Scientists have warned of the threat of pandemics, but business as usual triumphed. Poverty could have been eradicated over half a century ago but remains useful to the men in power.

I wondered what other catastrophes await us if we continue on the path set by our current leaders and what the future of leadership should entail. After learning more about the risks ahead, I felt I needed to do something—anything—to help improve our chances, so I started writing. This book contains a myriad of subjects. Though some may directly relate to leadership, they are things that everyone interested in leadership, thus humanity, should keep in mind. What is clear is that the leaders of today should not be the leaders of tomorrow. The time has come for self-serving men in office to step aside. A new era of leadership is emerging built on caring, compassion, and nonviolence, leaders who don't ask "What can you do for me?" but rather "What can I do for you?"

Chapter 1 will explore in more detail the threats that we face and why it is not alarmist or irrational to worry about human extinction in the coming century under our current leadership and trajectory, as very smart people whose job is to study existential threats now caution. Their warnings seem too outlandish to be true, but diving deeper into the subject provides terrifying insight into just how precarious our situation is.

Chapter 2 will explore the qualities that separate good leaders from bad. Our current predicament is the result of leadership choices over the last century. To get through the next 100 years, we urgently need to start making better choices. The chapter lists qualities that every leader, and everyone trying to pick a leader, should keep in mind, from the head of a small community-based organization to the CEO of a Fortune 500 company to a head of state.

Chapter 3 is about the surge of radical right-wing populist leaders around the world, including Donald Trump, Marine

Le Pen of France, Giorgia Meloni of Italy, and others. Jair Bolsonaro, on losing his reelection as president of Brazil, claimed, like Trump, to be the victim of fraud—a new normal for these leaders. The chapter describes the evolutionary traits and features that draw people to these leaders in times of crisis. It argues that like sugar cravings, they are something we need to resist. Few things could be as dangerous during this moment in history.

Chapter 4 will explore why we need a full representation of humanity—women, or more specifically, people with feminine qualities—in leadership positions. Last week, one of the wisest clients I have ever had the pleasure of working with asked me, "Can you coach me to be more like a man? I'm sick of not being seen or heard by my colleagues. I don't feel my skills are being valued. Why am I even here?" There it was again—the same dilemma I've heard countless times. Should I coach her to lower her voice, lean in and take up space, while striving to receive credit where credit isn't due? Surely, this would get her labeled a "bitch." But what is the alternative? Stay invisible? During our coaching session, she continued, "I don't even trust my own character and strengths as a woman." Here she hit the problem on the head: our leadership culture that doesn't value her. I know very well she is exactly what we need in leadership—a soft-spoken, incredibly wise person who values serving others and thrives in an environment of cooperation and collaboration. Globally in 2022, less than 9 percent of CEOs in the Fortune 500 were women. In politics, 12 percent of countries had a female head of state, and only 7 percent had achieved gender balance in cabinet positions.[21] In religion, 100 percent of the world's major religions were written by men and continue to be interpreted, organized, and led by men, including Buddhism, with the Dalai Lama the 14th being in a male-only lineage.

The quote "Hopefully, one day, women can become fully human beings when man gives her her freedom" is often attributed to the French poet Arthur Rimbaud over 150 years ago. Discussions on women's rights and freedom were far less common back then than they are today, yet the sentiment reflects a timeless understanding of the need for gender equality. Though the exact origin of this quote is unclear, it underscores the universal and ongoing struggle for women's liberation. Things are improving, but according to a 2022 UN report, at the current rate of progress it will take an estimated 300 years to end child marriage, 286 years to close gaps in legal protection and remove discriminatory laws, 140 years for women to be represented equally in positions of power and leadership in the workplace, and 47 years to achieve equal representation in national parliaments.[22] To put it bluntly, we live in a world where women, half of humanity, are not equally valued and empowered and the consequences are devastating; we simply don't have 300 years to get this right. Humanity will not reach its full potential until the skills of caring, compassion, and the wisdom of nonviolence that women bring are valued and equally incentivized.

Chapter 5 will provide thoughts about our education system and why it won't produce the leaders we need for the future. Historian Yuval Harari has argued, "The last thing a teacher needs is to give her pupils more information. They already have far too much of it. Instead, people need the ability to make sense of information, to tell the difference between what is important and what is unimportant, and above all to combine many bits of information into a broad picture of the world."[23] We also need to learn how to spot misinformation and fake news. The chapter will look more closely at Finland's education system as a model, with an emphasis on collaboration (a feminine quality) over competition (a masculine quality).

Chapter 6 will argue that we as a society need to rethink what we value and how to evaluate our priorities. In the Western world, we assume an unending correlation between income and happiness, but as we will see, having a high gross domestic product (GDP) or salary is not a prerequisite for well-being, nor does it guarantee it. Obsessing over GDP and making money has cost us our vision of what truly matters—long, meaningful, healthy lives.

The book will conclude with final thoughts on the road ahead and why wisdom, rather than simply intelligence, will be the difference between achieving a near-utopia or the end of the human story.

This book is about leadership at its core, and it contains a diverse range of related subjects. I could not have written it without the help of my research assistant David Lambert. Before partnering with me, David served as a research manager working with the United Nations Office of Dr. Paul Farmer, Special Adviser on Community Based Medicine and Lessons from Haiti. He has worked in Peru, Rwanda, Burundi, and Somalia. A large portion of this book is thanks to our long conversations together, helping illuminate the most pressing issues humanity faces in the coming decade and the new type of leadership in business and nations needed for humanity to prevail.

CHAPTER 1

What's at Stake

In 2017, *The New Yorker* published an article titled "Doomsday Prep for the Super-Rich." It highlighted a curious new hobby that had emerged among our most affluent citizens. Especially popular in Silicon Valley, billionaires, it seems, have begun preparing for the apocalypse. Helicopters on standby, luxury compounds in New Zealand, underground bunkers with air-filtration systems—these are the new toys for the super-rich. When asked to estimate what share of fellow Silicon Valley billionaires had acquired some level of "apocalypse insurance," in the form of a hideaway in the USA or abroad, Reid Hoffman, the co-founder of LinkedIn and a prominent investor, guessed 50 percent.[24]

Though most of us will never be able to afford a helicopter on standby, the survivalist craze is not confined to the super-rich. As the *New Yorker* article goes on to say, "In recent years, survivalism has been edging deeper into mainstream culture. In 2012, *National Geographic Channel* launched "Doomsday Preppers," a reality show featuring a series of Americans bracing for what they called S.H.T.F. (when the 'shit hits the fan')."

We enjoy reality TV shows like "Doomsday Preppers" where the characters are kooky and eccentric. We are amused by their paranoia, which at times borders on delusional. To most, they are simply reality TV show curiosities. As for billionaire survivalists constructing fortified compounds in the New Zealand wilderness, it seems to be a classic example of having more money than you know what to do with.

I have no plans to move my family to a remote compound stocked with canned goods and ammunition and did not write this book to convince you to. But if we are honest with ourselves, deep down I think that most of us share the same anxiety that is driving the survivalist craze, a feeling that something catastrophic is just around the corner. Anxiety and depression are on the rise; more than one out of every five Americans suffer from mental illness.[25] According to a study from researchers at Bath University in the UK that included 10,000 students in 10 countries between 16 and 25 years old, 60 percent believed the world is doomed and 40 percent do not want to have children because of it.[26] As the destruction of our environment continues, these numbers will only get worse given the link between pollution and mental health.

To put it simply, people everywhere worry about our prospects. Thinking of it in terms of an inflection point, most people assume we are heading to a steep downward trend as a species. This is strange since if you take a timeline of human history since, say, around 10,000 BC, the start of the agricultural revolution, and measure violent deaths, quality of life, life expectancy, infant mortality rates, and most other metrics of well-being, it would appear that we have already hit the inflection point and are headed in the right direction. As anthropologist Rutger Bregman observes in his excellent book *Humankind,* "Only in the last two centuries—the blink of an eye—have things got better so quickly that we've forgotten how abysmal life used to be. If you take the history of civilization and clock it over twenty-four hours, the first twenty-three hours and forty-five minutes would be sheer misery."[27]

If anything, we should be thrilled. The prophets of positivity like to point to human psychology and the media as the reason people are so gloomy. In *The Better Angels of Our Nature*, Steven Pinker argues, "Our cognitive faculties predispose us to believe that we live in violent times, especially when they are stoked by media that follow the watchword 'if it bleeds, it leads.' The human mind tends to estimate the probability of an event from the ease with which it can recall examples. Scenes of carnage are more likely to be beamed into our homes and burned into our memories than footage of people dying of old age."[28]

I did not write this book to criticize the Steven Pinkers and Hans Roslings of the world. Compared with the past, the world is an astoundingly good place and this progress is worth celebrating. Their explanations of why people are pessimistic make sense: I would be shocked if things like media sensationalism don't give people a negatively skewed view of things. In a 2015 study, a team of media researchers compiled data from over four million news items on immigration, crime, and terrorism to determine if there were any patterns. What they found was that in times when immigration or violence decline, newspapers give them more coverage. "Hence," they concluded, "there seems to be none or even a negative relationship between news and reality."[29]

But we are approaching the most consequential inflection point in human history and we need to rethink our conception of leadership to stand a chance. As author John Maxwell once said, "Everything rises and falls on leadership."[30] Part of convincing you of this too means first telling you why, despite all the recent positive trends highlighted by Pinker and Rosling, things could get very bad, very quickly.

For the past 14 years, I have been closely involved in efforts to raise awareness about climate change. The frustration I felt over the failure of world leaders to take meaningful action was what initially motivated this book. But I am not a climatologist and won't be releasing any new findings—there are also writers far more knowledgeable and eloquent than I am on the subject, like Elizabeth Kolbert with her Pulitzer Prize-winning book *The Sixth Extinction*, or my colleague, former director at the National Oceanic and Atmospheric Administration (NOAA), Alexander MacDonald, whose book *Saving Paradise* will be released soon. The purpose of this chapter is not to argue that unless we demand that our leaders take serious action on climate change, a looming disaster will threaten civilization. There is hope, a lot of it, but things need to change, and change fast.

As schoolchildren, we learn that an asteroid was what killed the dinosaurs. When we begin to get a bit older, it dawns on us that the same thing could happen to humans. By this point, most of us have already struggled with the realization that our own lives and those of the people we love could end any day through chance occurrences. But the end of the human story? We immediately recognize that as something not to think about.

As we get older still, we hear about nuclear weapons and what they are capable of. Especially for anyone who, like me, grew up during the height of the Cold War when a nuclear confrontation between the two great powers seemed inevitable, not thinking about it was almost a prerequisite for sanity. We don't want to think about the end of humanity—the end of culture, the end of science, and the end of the lives of all of our ancestors who contributed to the future of their descendants. "Extinction is the undoing of the human enterprise," wrote American atronomer and planetary scientist Carl Sagan.[31] The thought is too much for most of us to bear, so we put it in the back of our minds and tell ourselves that the end of the human story won't come for millions, perhaps billions, of years; it is not something to worry about.

But one person who does worry about it is the philosopher Toby Ord of Oxford University. Ord is a pioneer in a curious new academic discipline that has emerged in the last few decades. I call it doomsday scholarship, though Ord prefers the less dramatic term "existential risk," often shortened to "X-risk" among the community of scholars and activists inspired by Ord's pioneering work.

In 2010, Ord along with his friend and colleague Nick Bostrom founded the Future of Humanity Institute (FHI) based out of Oxford University. FHI was a multidisciplinary research center composed of some of the world's most influential mathematicians, philosophers, computer scientists, engineers, political scientists, and economists working together to explore "big-picture questions for civilization."

A primary component of FHIs' research agenda was estimating the probability of different existential risks, which it defined as follows:

Existential risk: A risk that destroys humanity's long-term potential in terms of technological progress and standards of living.

FHI classified risks of human extinction by the three successive stages that need to occur before we go extinct:

1. Origin: How does the catastrophe get started?

2. Scaling: How does the catastrophe reach a global scale?

3. Endgame: How does the catastrophe finish the job?

This classification breaks down the probability of extinction into the product of (1) the probability it gets started, (2) the probability it reaches a global scale given it gets started, and (3) the probability it causes extinction given it reaches a global scale:

$$P \text{ extinction} = P \text{ origin} \times P \text{ scaling} \times P \text{ endgame}$$

Asteroids

For some good news, FHI factored this information into its equation and came up with the estimate that the chances of an asteroid causing our extinction in the next 100 years is 1 in 1,000,000, about the same as getting hit by lightning. The low odds are thanks to the low probability that the catastrophe will ever get started in the first place (origin). So if the movie *Armageddon* made you anxious, you can breathe a sigh of relief: We don't have much to fear from asteroids, and not because Bruce Willis will be there to nuke them.

Now for the bad news: the reality is much more terrifying. The experts at FHI estimated the chances of us not making it through the next century as one in six. This is 17 percent. Imagine being forced to fly in a plane that had a 17 percent chance of crashing in a fiery wreck. Now imagine that everyone you love is on it too. How much would you pay to decrease the odds of it crashing by, say, 10 percent? As a mother of two, my answer is whatever it costs. If you are like me, it doesn't make much difference when considering the life of everyone on the planet as well, because ensuring the safety of your loved ones alone is worth whatever the costs.

And we haven't begun to consider the lives of those who haven't been born yet. As Ord argues, every person holds equal value, no matter when they exist. Our lives are just as meaningful as those who lived millennia ago or those who will live millennia from now. Just as it is wrong to believe that people physically further away matter less, it is equally wrong to think people chronologically further away matter less. The importance of their happiness and the severity of their suffering remain undiminished.[32]

For every potential existential catastrophe, the experts at FHI employed sophisticated techniques to predict the probability of each of the three stages, spending months incorporating as much data and evidence into them as possible with input from the world's leading experts in a myriad of fields. Still, even with a risk as well characterized as asteroid impacts, the scientific evidence only takes us part of the way: we have good evidence regarding the chance of impact (origin) but not on the chance a given impact will destroy our future (endgame). As Ord acknowledges, "There is significant uncertainty remaining in these estimates."[33]

Naturally, I first assumed the 17 percent estimate was a result of this uncertainty being filled with alarmist predictions. But now I think it may be too optimistic.

Climate Change

What is it that has experts like Ord so worried? Climate change is, of course, on the list and was considered by FHI to be one of the "big five" existential risks.

The planet has heated considerably since the start of the Industrial Revolution in the late 1800s, when humans began burning massive quantities of fossil fuels, releasing carbon dioxide (CO_2). For the past sixty or so million years, the concentration of CO_2 in the atmosphere has slowly increased at an annual rate of about 0.00001 parts per million (PPM). In the past 30 years, it has gone up by 100 PPM.

What's Warming the World?
Global temperature change since 1850 (°C)

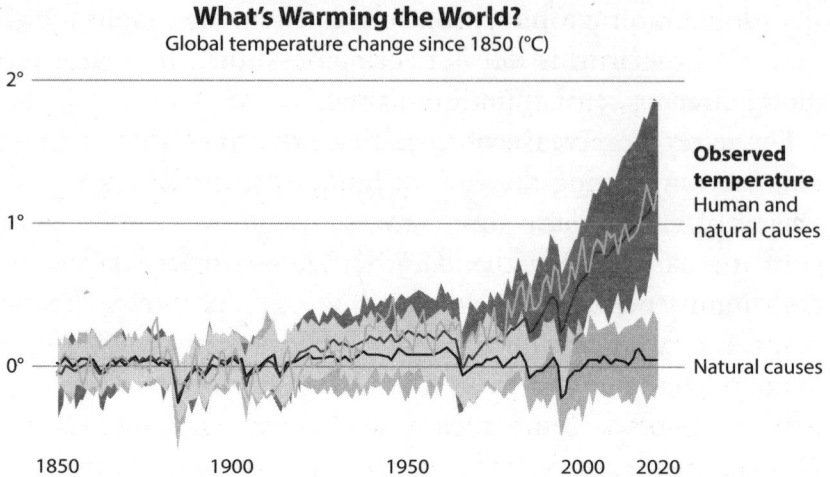

Figure 1.1 What's warming the world: Global temperature change since 1850 (°C) (*Source*: Climate Central[34])

As physicist Aatish Bhatia notes:

> Here's an astonishing fact: humans have pumped more carbon dioxide into the air in my lifetime than in the time between my birth and the start of the Industrial Revolution. If you look at all carbon dioxide added to the atmosphere since the Industrial Revolution, more than half was added *after 1990*. A quarter was added *after 2007*. Just 30 years—a single generation—accounts for half of all carbon emissions in the history of burning fossil fuels.[35]

CO_2 is a greenhouse gas, meaning it is more transparent to the incoming light from the Sun than it is to the heat that radiates back from the Earth. It acts like a blanket: trapping some of the heat and keeping the Earth warm. Since 1880, the global average temperature has risen by roughly 1.8°F (1°C).[36] Though this doesn't seem like much, it creates dramatic changes. Just think about when you have a fever and a temperature increase of just 1°C, how does that feel? For comparison, during the last ice age 20,000 years ago, Earth was only 5°C colder.

In an example of the lengths some media outlets will go to mislead the public, in 2015, the *National Review* magazine tweeted a line graph with the caption "The only #climatechange chart you need to see." It was titled "Average Annual Global Temperature in Fahrenheit 1880–2015", with temperature on the vertical axis ranging from -10 to 110°F and years on the horizontal axis from 1880 to 2015. The temperature line appeared nearly flat, hovering around 56 to 58°F.

By setting the upper and lower boundaries of the chart at 110°F (43°C) and -10°F (-23°C) respectively—two extremes that the planet won't get anywhere near before the catastrophic effects of climate change take effect with even a 1°F rise in global average temperature—the *National Review* was essentially zooming so far out on the problem that it's impossible to see.

It appears that the *National Review* has since deleted this tweet. However, the misleading nature of this graph was widely reported and commented on at the time so the graph and screenshots of the tweet have been archived on other sites.[37]

For anyone not willingly blind to the problem, repercussions are clear. As Figure 1.2 shows, the *ten hottest years ever* have all taken place since 2010. Each year the situation grows more dire—this book was edited after the summer of 2024, the new record holder for the hottest year in human history, breaking the record from 2023.[38]

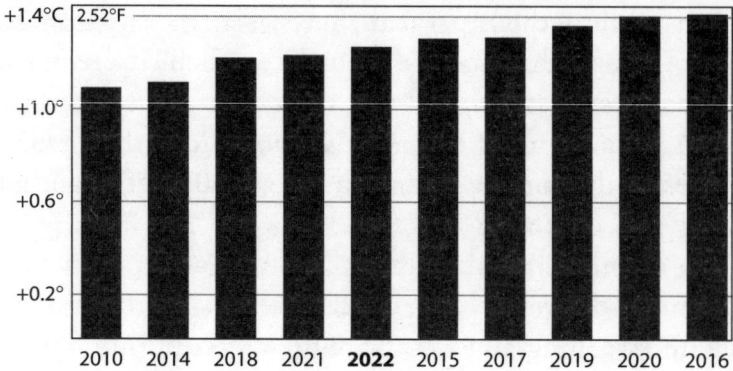

Figure 1.2 The 10 hottest years in human history
(*Source*: Climate Central)[39]

The year 2025 started out with devastating wildfires in Los Angeles. Twenty-nine people lost their lives, 18,000 structures were destroyed or damaged and tens of thousands of people were forced from their homes. One of the victims was Anthony Mitchell who was wheelchair bound and refused to leave his son Justin behind, who had cerebral palsy and couldn't walk. Anthony was found dead alongside his beloved son.[40] In the United States, wildfires are the most conspicuous consequence of climate change.[41] A study found that a 1.8 °F (1°C) increase in the mean summer temperature raises the risk of starting a fire—either by human activity or a lightning strike—by 19–22 percent and increases burned land by 22–25 percent.[42]

In the western United States, where I live, the number of major fires doubled between 1984 and 2015. Colorado's fresh mountain air is often filled with smoke as wildfires burn out of control. Not long ago I read an article about Chris O'Brien, the chief firefighter at my local fire department, who fought his first fire in 1989. "Fires today are not the fires we trained for," he explains. "Their intensity is out of control.

They don't follow the historical characteristics of wildfires in Colorado. They scare me."[43]

Wildfires are becoming a serious problem in my homeland as well. The worst wildfires in Sweden's history took place in 2018 during a record-breaking heatwave, with the warmest May and July ever recorded, with 60 wildfires, including 11 above the Arctic Circle.[44] When I was a child, 90°F (32.2°C) days above the Arctic Circle were unheard of. These days, people are installing air conditioning.

In October 2020, my family was evacuated from two locations and the neighborhood just north of us burned down. During fire season, I see palpable anxiety in my children as outdoor activities are canceled due to the smoke and the possibility looms that we will need to evacuate. Yesterday, while working on this book, we were placed on high alert—and it isn't even summer. It is exhausting. In December 2021, when Colorado should have been covered in snow, 1,084 homes just south of Boulder burned down in the Marshall Fire. But Coloradoans and Californians are the lucky ones. Though we should never dismiss the suffering of anyone who loses their home, climate change has much more dire consequences for hundreds of millions of people around the world, According to the United Nations Refugee Agency, UNHCR, 21.5 million people were considered climate-related refugees in 2021, and according to Zurich Insurance Group, that number will be closer to 1.2 billion by 2050.[45] Where are they all going to go? Another heartbreaking statistic, often overlooked, is the effect of wildfires on animals and their habitats. In the wildfires that swept Australia in 2019–2020, more than three billion animals lost their lives, and it is anyone's guess as to how many were displaced.[46]

I recently sat down with Linda Mearns, one of the authors of the Intergovernmental Panel on Climate Change (IPCC) Report. As she put it, "One thing is for sure, there is going to be a lot of suffering."[47] The number of people who go hungry, which the UN's Food and Agriculture Organization (FAO) defines as having not enough caloric intake to meet daily minimum energy requirements, is rising. Since 1970, the percentage of people living in developing countries who go hungry has decreased from 35 percent of the population to less than 15 percent.[48] In 2000, the UN set a goal of eliminating world hunger by 2030. This was an ambitious goal, but for most of the twenty-first century we seemed to be on track to accomplish it. In the past few years, however, something went wrong.

In July 2021, the UN released its annual report "The State of Food Security and Nutrition in the World" showing that 118 million more people went hungry in 2020 than in 2019. This was a horrifying increase after decades of progress.[49] The sharp spike in 2020 can be attributed to Covid-19, but as Figures 1.3 and 1.4 show, progress in eliminating world hunger began to stall in 2017 before steadily reversing.

Quoting Alexander MacDonald, "The existence of extreme poverty unsolved in the wealthy twenty-first century is an

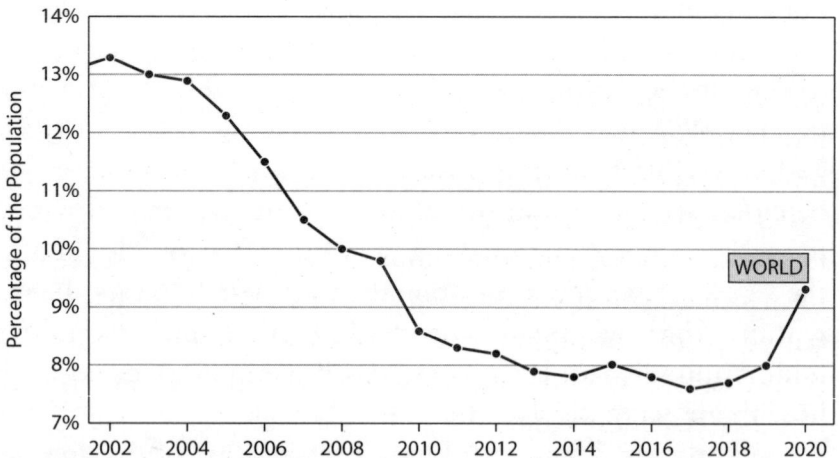

Figure 1.3 Prevalence of undernourishment as a percentage of the population between 2002 and 2020 (*Source*: World Bank)[50]

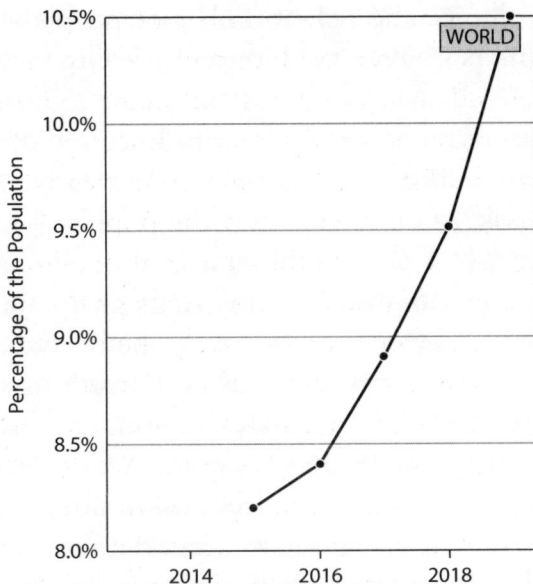

Figure 1.4 Percentage of the population facing food insecurity—defined as when a person's life or livelihood is in immediate danger because of lack of food—since 2015[51]

ethical failure of humanity." Like climate change, we know, through many scientists including Buckminster Fuller, that the world produces enough food to feed everyone on this planet. We have the resources to end poverty. It won't be easy, but we also know how to do it. What we don't have, however, is the will of the men in power.

Perhaps what is most horrifying is that there is a time lag between CO_2 emissions and the full heating effect. This means that even if we stopped emitting CO_2 entirely, the hot temperatures, droughts, fires, hurricanes, floods, and other repercussions would continue for a decade or so before getting better. Unnervingly, we are not even close to stopping CO_2 emissions; in fact, we are increasing the *rate* at which we add CO_2 into the atmosphere way outside the safe target of a 2.7°F (1.5°C) increase set by the Paris Agreement.[52]

Is climate change the reason FHI estimated that we have only a one in six chance of making it through the century? According to Ord, what is concerning about climate change is that our human activities today can lock in disasters in the future. In turn leading to an existential catastrophe. Due to this serious risk, climate change should be considered even more important to fight and mitigate.[53]

What concerns doomsday scholars like Ord the most are "feedback loops." A feedback loop is the equivalent of a vicious or virtuous circle—something that accelerates or decelerates a warming trend. Positive feedback accelerates a temperature rise, whereas negative feedback decelerates it. Scientists are aware of a number of positive feedback loops in the climate system. One example is melting ice. Because ice is light-colored and reflective, a large proportion of the sunlight that hits it is bounced back to space, which limits the amount of warming it causes. But as the world gets warmer, ice melts, revealing the darker-colored land or water below. The result is that more of the Sun's energy is absorbed, leading to more warming, which in turn leads to more ice melting, and so on. According to Ord, "We hear of warming producing further warming and our thoughts naturally turn to a world spinning out of control."[54]

We know with certainty that climate change has started (origin) and it has global effects (scaling). But we don't know the endgame yet. For climate change to be considered an existential catastrophe, it would need to either completely wipe out the human race in the next 100 years or lock us into the point of no possible return. There are scenarios where this is possible. Yet because of the low probability of an endgame, FHI estimated that there is "only" a 1 in 1,000 chance of climate change causing an existential catastrophe in the next 100 years.

0.001 extinction = 1.0 origin × 1.0 scaling × 0.001 endgame

It is important not to misinterpret this. Climate change is not the most serious *existential* risk we face, according to FHI. But this does not mean that it is not the most urgent and serious problem we face. Doomsday scholars divide existential risks and global catastrophic risks. In the introduction to the cheerful *Global Catastrophic Risks*, Bostrom provides the following definition:

Global catastrophic risk: *A risk that might have the potential to inflict serious damage to human well-being on a global scale.*[55]

As a reminder, the definition of existential risk that Ord provides in *The Precipice* and what FHI was referring to in its estimate is:

Existential risk: *A risk that destroys humanity's long-term potential in terms of technological progress and standards of living.*[56]

Climate change is better thought of as a global catastrophic risk. For anyone not familiar with the lingo, it is natural to assume that global catastrophic risks are bad, but existential risks are worse. Technically speaking, however, an existential risk doesn't necessarily even need to be a bad thing.

Confused?

When coming up with their estimate for climate change, the experts at FHI concluded that even in many worst-case scenarios, parts of the Earth would remain habitable and some humans could likely find a way to survive. Though humanity may find itself in a *Mad Max*-like world because of climate change, as long as there are some humans around, our "*long-term* potential" remains intact. Because climate change is already happening, it has an origin of 1.0, making it the most serious global catastrophe we face. The fact that doomsday scholars calculate it has a 1 in 1,000 chance of causing our extinction should not obscure this fact.

As Ord argues, without cutting our carbon emissions, climate change would be an "unparalleled human and environmental tragedy, forcing mass migration and starvation. This is reason enough to do our utmost to prevent anything like that from ever happening."[57]

Of course, climate change is not the only form of environmental damage we are inflicting upon the Earth. We face other environmental existential risks, including overpopulation, running out of critical resources, and biodiversity loss. Environmental catastrophes such as these are grouped to make up another of the "big five" existential risks. According to FHI's estimate, there is the same probability of one causing our extinction in the coming century as climate change.[58]

As with extreme global warming, we don't know of a direct mechanism for existential risk from other potential environmental catastrophes, but we are putting such pressure on the global environment that there may well be unknown consequences that would threaten our survival. We could therefore think of continuing environmental damage over the coming century as a source of unforeseen threats to humanity.

The simple truth is that climate change and other environmental issues are leading the world to a dystopia of untold suffering—and society is oddly confused about this despite what is right in front of their eyes. In 2005, British Petroleum (BP) ingeniously coined the term "carbon footprint" to divert attention from the fossil fuel industry and place blame on individuals for climate change. This strategic move successfully shifted public focus toward personal choices, allowing the industry to continue its environmentally damaging practices unchecked.

The practical implications of BP's "carbon footprint" campaign are evident in the daily struggles of a busy parent, like myself, juggling work, family, and health. Amidst the chaos, reusable items are forgotten, plastic is used, and the guilt of contributing to a "carbon footprint" sets in. This internalized blame leaves little energy for activism or engagement in anti-fossil fuel efforts.[59]

While personal responsibility is essential, it should not overshadow the real culprits—the fossil fuel industry. Only 100 companies are responsible for 70 percent of global emissions and our focus should be on holding them accountable. Urgent impact is needed, thus it must come from the top down, with these companies transitioning to renewable energy sources.[60]

Ironically, renewable energy is not only environmentally friendly but also less expensive and more reliable. The solution lies in a rapid shift toward renewable energy and a transformation of the entire economy. The time for change is now, and the power to make it happen rests with these influential companies. Rather than dwelling on individual choices like plastic straws, we must channel our efforts toward collective action. Signing petitions, contacting legislators, participating in anti-fossil fuel demonstrations, and actively engaging in the voting process are the key steps toward a sustainable future. Let's redirect our focus and demand accountability from those truly responsible for the climate crisis: the fossil fuel giants.

We need leaders willing and able to recognize these things. The fact that "endgame" scenarios are difficult to envision shouldn't be a source of comfort for anyone. But it does raise the question, if the environment isn't the reason for our one in six chances in the decades ahead, what is? What could "finish the job"?

Nuclear Weapons

In 1945, the bloodiest years in human history came to an end. But the euphoria that peace brought to a war-weary world soon gave way to a disturbing realization: If there was a third world war, there wouldn't be a fourth.

Anyone who grew up during the Cold War is well aware that nuclear weapons represented an unprecedented threat to humanity. In a display of collective insanity, the USA and the USSR had thousands of them pointed at each other, a hair-trigger away from mutually assured destruction. What most people don't know is how close it actually came.

One example came on a Saturday in October 1962 as the Cuban Missile Crisis was cascading out of control. US warships enforcing the blockade of Cuba detected a Soviet submarine and attempted to force it to the surface by dropping low-explosive depth charges as warning shots. The submarine was out of radio contact and its crew had no idea if a war was already happening. A broken ventilator raised the temperature to 140°F (60°C) in some parts of the sub, causing crew members to fall unconscious as depth charges exploded near the hull.

Desperate, the captain decided to unleash the submarine's secret weapon—a nuclear missile. The submarine's political officer, who held the other half of the firing key, gave his consent. On any other submarine in Cuban waters that day, the weapon would have been fired. Fortunately, a man named Vasili Arkhipov was on the sub. Arkhipov was the commander of the entire flotilla and by sheer luck happened to be on that particular submarine. He talked the captain down from his rage and persuaded him to await further orders from Moscow.

These events were declassified in 2002. Fifteen years later, in 2017, the Future of Life Institute, a non-profit that advocates for the reduction of existential risks, posthumously presented Arkhipov the first "Future of Life Award" in recognition of exceptional measures to safeguard the collective future of humanity. He also had a room at FHI named in his honor.[61]

In the aftermath of the Cuban Missile Crisis, President Kennedy and Soviet premier Khrushchev took steps to mitigate the risk posed by nuclear weapons. A direct telephone link between the White House and the Kremlin, known as the "Hotline," was installed to prevent any "misunderstandings" from destroying the human race. Having approached the brink of nuclear conflict, both superpowers also began to reconsider the nuclear arms race and took the first steps in agreeing to the Test Ban Treaty, which was signed by 123 states on August 5, 1963 in Moscow, the Soviet Union.

Though the size of the nuclear arsenals has declined from a peak of 70,000 in 1986 to about 14,000 today, nuclear weapons remain a serious threat to humanity.[62] Recent years have witnessed the emergence of new geopolitical tensions that may again raise the risks of deliberate war—between the old superpowers and new ones. We have witnessed the collapse of key arms-control mechanisms between the USA and Russia. And there are worrying signs that these tensions may restart the arms race, increasing the number and size of weapons toward the old levels or beyond.

Worries of a nuclear confrontation with Russia were, of course, compounded in February 2022 with its invasion of Ukraine. Within a week of the invasion, Russian President Vladimir Putin said he was "forced" into the decision to put nuclear forces on special alert as a result of "aggressive statements" made by the West.[63]

To most people, myself included, asteroids, climate change, and nuclear weapons seemed like the only real existential risks to worry about. Surprisingly, however, nuclear war was not the biggest reason for FHI's one in six estimates either. It is, however, one of the "big five" with a 1 in 1,000 existential risk.

Nuclear weapons are a technological marvel and humanity's first invention powerful enough to cause our own extinction. Fortunately, they require several kilograms of plutonium or highly enriched uranium, both of which are very difficult and expensive to produce. But suppose it had turned out otherwise, that there had been some really easy way to unleash the energy of the atom. Let's say by sending an electric current through a metal object placed between two sheets of glass. In his "vulnerable world hypothesis," Oxford philosopher Nick Bostrom urges us to imagine technology as balls in an urn. There are white balls, which represent technologies that are purely beneficial for society, such as vaccines. There are gray balls representing technologies that are a mixed blessing or with containable risks, like nuclear weapons. And then there are black balls. These are technologies that invariably or by default destroy the civilization that invents them. "Easy nukes" are a hypothetical example of a black ball discovery. Since you are reading this, we haven't pulled one out. But as Bostrom observes, "The reason is not that we have been particularly careful or wise in our technology policy. We have just been lucky."[64]

The two final and most probable of the "big five" existential risks are potential black balls. As we will see, unless we fundamentally rethink leadership, our luck will run out as the gap between our power and our wisdom grows at an accelerating rate.

Engineered Pandemics

On the morning of March 20, 1995, five men entered the Tokyo subway system. After boarding separate subway lines, they continued for several stops before dropping the bags they were carrying and exiting. An odorless, colorless liquid inside the bags began to vaporize. Within minutes, commuters began choking and vomiting. The trains continued toward the heart of Tokyo, with sick passengers leaving the cars at each station. The fumes were spread at each stop, either by emanating from the tainted cars or through contact with people's clothing and shoes. By the end of the day, 13 people lay dead and 5,800 were seriously injured.

The group responsible for the attack was the religious cult Aum Shinrikyo. Its motive for murdering innocent people? To bring about the end of the world.

Aum Shinrikyo, which remains active with an estimated 2,000 followers as of 2020, believes that the end of the world is imminent and only a few elites (themselves) will survive. The 1995 attack was intended to kick-start the apocalypse.[65]

The concern is not Aum Shinrikyo—though we can all agree they would not be missed. Whether part of a group like ISIS or a "lone wolf," there will always be people who want to inflict mass murder for whatever delusion. As the Tokyo attack illustrated, there are even those with the explicit goal of bringing on the apocalypse. What concerned FHI researchers was that biotechnology may soon offer them a means.

Our understanding of pandemics and medicine may have increased, but as Covid-19 has proven, the world can still be brought to its knees by infectious diseases. As of August 2023, Covid-19 had infected more than 770 million people and killed over 7 million. No other event since World War II impacted us on such a global scale. But no matter how bad it seemed, we need to keep in mind that it could have been much worse.

Mark Woolhouse and Eleanor Gaunt of the University of Edinburgh estimate there are about 1,400 human pathogens out there and about 150 of those have epidemic potential. We've been fighting the same dozen or so bacteria, fungi, and viruses ever since we began aggregating in communities large enough for germs to take hold and multiply. As we keep encroaching on nature, we can expect to continue encountering new and deadly pathogens that jump from wild animals to humans.[66]

Interestingly, FHI classified "natural" pandemics as an anthropogenic risk. Modern civilization makes it much easier for a pandemic to spread. The higher density of people living together in cities increases the number of people each of us may infect. Rapid long-distance transport greatly increases the distance pathogens can spread, reducing the degrees of separation between any two people. Moreover, we are no longer divided into isolated populations as we were for most of the last 10,000 years. Together these effects suggest that we might expect more new pandemics to spread more quickly and to reach a higher percentage of the world's population. FHI estimated that the chances of a natural pandemic leading to an existential catastrophe in the next 100 years is 1 in 10,000.[67]

But it is not naturally occurring pandemics that should concern us the most. Humanity has a long and dark history of weaponizing disease, with records dating back to 1320 BC describing a war in Asia Minor when infected sheep were driven across the border to spread tularemia (also known as rabbit fever, an infectious disease caused by bacteria found in ticks, deer flies, and other infected animals). During the twentieth century, 15 countries are known to have developed bioweapons programs, attempting to weaponize diseases to make them deadlier. While there is no evidence of deliberate attempts to create a pathogen to threaten the whole of humanity, the logic of deterrence or mutually assured destruction could push superpowers or rogue states in that direction.

State-sponsored bioweapon programs are dangerous and should be eradicated. Overall, however, biological warfare has become taboo among nations. Today, only 6 countries are known to have continuing programs, down from 15 during the height of the Cold War.

The problem is that soon groups like Aum Shinrikyo, or even a moderately intelligent "lone wolf" psychopath could create a virus far more lethal and contagious than anything Cold War-era superpowers could have dreamed of.

One of the most exciting trends in biotechnology is its rapid progress and the speed at which cutting-edge techniques can be adopted by students and amateurs. As genome engineering technologies become more powerful and universal, the tools necessary for making these modifications will become increasingly accessible. Just 75 years ago, we were not even confident that DNA was the primary material governing genetic heredity. Today, we can read, write, and edit genomes with increasing ease. When a breakthrough is achieved, the pool of people with the talent, training, and resources to reproduce it rapidly expands: from a handful of the world's top biologists to people with PhDs in the field, to millions of people with undergraduate-level biology. It is estimated that there are 30,000 people with the talent, training, and access to technology to create new pathogens. This figure could rapidly expand. Gene synthesis, which allows the creation of custom biological agents, has dropped steeply in price, with its cost halving approximately every 15 months. Furthermore, with the arrival of benchtop DNA synthesis machines, access will become much easier and could avoid existing gene synthesis screening efforts, which complicates controlling the spread of such technology.

Even with just our current capabilities, an engineered pandemic could join the growing list of seismic changes made possible by biotechnological advances. Sufficiently capable actors—like Aum Shinrikyo, which is reported to have millions of dollars and "brilliant young scientists" at its disposal—could work to resurrect the deadliest pathogens of the past, like smallpox or Spanish flu, or modify existing ones such as bird flu, making them more contagious and lethal.

This leads to the terrifying specter of independent actors intentionally (or unintentionally) engineering pathogens with the potential to inflict worse harm than history's deadliest pandemics. No obvious physical or biological constraints preclude the construction of such potent biological weapons. According to biosecurity expert Piers Millett, "If you're deliberately trying to create a pathogen that is deadly, spreads easily, and that we don't have appropriate public health measures to mitigate, then that thing you create is amongst the most dangerous things on the planet."[68]

It may be possible for the scientific community to overcome these challenges and provide strong management of global risks, but it would require a willingness to accept serious changes to its culture, its governance, and, most importantly, its leadership before catastrophe strikes.

According to FHI's estimates, there is a 1 in 30 chance of an engineered pandemic causing an existential catastrophe in the coming century. There was only one thing that its researchers were more afraid of.[69]

Artificial Intelligence (AI)

The most serious risk humanity faces according to FHI—with a 1 in 10 chance of causing our extinction this century—is also the most outlandish sounding.[70] For most people, when they hear of AI and extinction, the first images in their head are from *The Terminator* or *The Matrix*. Researchers such as Ord and Bostrom hate this because it makes the issue sound less like science and more like science fiction. I was certainly guilty of thinking so. But these movies in no way represent the actual threat, which is more frightening than anything Hollywood has dreamed of.

There are three calibers of AI:

1. Artificial Narrow Intelligence (ANI): This is an AI that specializes in one task and can easily outperform any human.

For example, in 1996, IBM's Deep Blue played world champion Garry Kasparov in a six-game match, losing four games to two. The next year, after a few upgrades, a rematch took place, with Deep Blue defeating Kasparov by winning three games and drawing one (though there is speculation that IBM broke the rules by using human players to improve Deep Blue's strategy during the game). Deep Blue was one of the world's most powerful supercomputers at the time. Today, five-time World Chess Champion Magnus Carlsen wouldn't stand a chance against your smartphone while you watched YouTube videos on it.

2. Artificial General Intelligence (AGI): This is a system that could outperform humans in any intellectual competition.

3. Artificial Super Intelligence (ASI): Finally, we get to ASI. Bostrom defines superintelligence as "an intellect that is much smarter than the best human brains in practically every field, including scientific creativity, general wisdom, and social skills." By much smarter, Bostrom is comparing Stephen Hawking to a grasshopper.[71]

The world runs on ANI (your phone could beat Carlsen at chess and checkers because it relies on different apps which are the source of the intelligence) and full AGI is likely just around the corner.

Deep Blue was specifically programmed to play chess. IBM's programmers built a function that incorporated detailed chess knowledge to evaluate any given board position. They used IBM's supercomputer to search 200 million moves per second to calculate the best ones. This is what is known as "brute force." (One of the reasons IBM was suspected of cheating was that some of Deep Blue's moves showed creativity and risk rather than the boring, methodological style that was synonymous with computer chess).

Deep Blue had an estimated Elo rating—a method of calculating the skill of players—of around 2,700–2,750. To put this in perspective, Magnus Carlsen has an Elo of 2,882, the highest any human has obtained. A program called Stockfish, which is essentially an updated version of Deep Blue, has one of 3,475. The difference between it and Carlsen is about the same as a professional player and a strong club player. This is certainly impressive, but Stockfish doesn't keep Bostrom up at night. There isn't any mystery to how it works, making it no more of an X-risk than your calculator. The system that dethroned Stockfish, however, is an entirely different agent.

As of 2022, the best chess player in history was AlphaZero, which was developed by DeepMind, a company owned by Google. Unlike Stockfish and Deep Blue, which use brute-force calculations learning derived from human experience, AlphaZero relies on artificial neural networks (ANNs) and deep learning algorithms. ANNs are inspired by the human brain, mimicking the way that biological neurons signal to one another. AlphaZero is provided with no knowledge of chess beyond the basic rules of the game. It then begins to play itself millions of times an hour using random moves and taking note of what moves win and lose. It took two hours before it began beating typical human players. After four hours, it reached an Elo rating of 3,575, which is 100 higher than Stockfish, the equivalent of the world's number one ranked player and the fiftieth. What was even more exciting was that it didn't play with the boring, methodological style of Stockfish and Deep Blue, but instead showed the creativity and daringness of human players. The most important thing about AlphaZero, however, is that it can do more than play chess.

The ancient game of Go originated in China 3,000 years ago and occupies the same cultural space as chess does in the West. Two players, using either white or black stones, take turns placing their stones on a board. The goal is to surround and capture their opponent's stones or strategically create spaces of territory. Once all possible moves have been played, both the stones on the board and the empty points are tallied. The highest number wins.

Though the rules are simple, Go is profoundly complex. There are an astonishing 10^170 possible board configurations (a 1 followed by 170 zeros). To put this in perspective, the number of atoms in the universe is around 10^78. The game is much more intuitive than chess and using the brute-force method allows machines to reach the level of a strong amateur player.

In March 2016, a match reminiscent of the Kasparov and Deep Blue match 20 years earlier took place between AlphaZero and Lee Sedol, the world's best Go player. "I believe that human intuition is still too advanced for AI to have caught up," Sedol noted before the game. Stunningly, after first playing itself for eight hours, AlphaZero defeated Sedol. The world's best Go players had thought their play was close to perfection. "After humanity spent thousands of years improving our tactics, computers tell us that humans are completely wrong," said Kin Jue, another top-ranked player. "I would go as far as to say not a single human has touched the edge of the truth of Go."[72]

In our world, "less intelligent" is an IQ of around 85, average is 100, and genius is above 140. A handful of individuals possess IQs of 180 to 200. What would something thousands of times more intelligent be like? We have no way of comprehending this. Seemingly impossible problems such as traveling faster than the speed of light could be as obvious as flipping on a light switch. Overnight, it could find a cure for cancer, solve climate change, or provide humans with the gift of eternal life. The problem, of course, is that ending life would be just as simple.

Unsurprisingly, one person who isn't concerned about AI is Steven Pinker, who claimed, "We do know that it's possible to have high intelligence without megalomaniacal, homicidal, or genocidal tendencies ... they're called women"—something we will explore in Chapter 4.[73] What Pinker fails to understand is that the AI wouldn't need to be any more genocidal than someone removing an ant colony on their front lawn.

In 1981, philosopher Peter Singer published a book called *The Expanding Circle*.[74] It argues that throughout human history, people have steadily expanded the circle of those who deserve compassion and dignity. When we started out, it included oneself, family, and tribe. Eventually, people decided that perhaps others in their settlements deserved the same. Soon this expanded again, to those of the same nationality, race, and so on, eventually encircling humanity as a whole. Needless to say, this hasn't guaranteed compassion and dignity, but if the mayor of modern-day Athens announced his intention to enslave the residents of Peloponnese, Athenians would certainly be more against the idea than they were in 400 BC. We have even recently begun caring about the suffering of highly intelligent non-human animals like chimps and dolphins. According to Singer, eventually, the circle will expand to all beings capable of suffering and things like factory farms will be seen as shameful remnants of the past, much like slave plantations are viewed today.

Pigs, emblematic of animals subjected to systemic cruelty, possess a level of intelligence and social complexity comparable to dogs. They are capable of recognizing their names, responding to commands, and forming intricate social bonds. Yet, in the stark reality of industrial agriculture, pigs and their offspring are confined in egregiously small cages, barely accommodating their bodies, and piglets are routinely separated from their mothers shortly after birth. This treatment is not an isolated incident but a widespread practice within a profit-driven capitalist system, where economic considerations often override ethical concerns. The pursuit of minimizing costs and maximizing profits dictates conditions that are fundamentally at odds with the well-being of these sentient creatures.

The grim reality extends beyond pigs to encompass the 75 billion domesticated animals living and dying in unspeakable agony in factory farming, including cows, chickens, goats, and sheep, all raised and slaughtered to satisfy human consumption of meat. An estimated 18 billion of these animals perish prematurely due to inadequate living conditions, transportation stress, or as casualties of the inefficiencies inherent in food production and distribution.[75] Moreover, the environmental degradation associated with animal agriculture—exemplified by excessive water usage, land exploitation, and the substantial contributions to greenhouse gas emissions—further underscores the unsustainability and ethical bankruptcy of current practices.

This critical examination of our treatment of animals within the agricultural system reveals not only the immense suffering inflicted upon sentient beings but also the profound environmental consequences of perpetuating such practices. It challenges us to reconsider the ethical implications of our dietary choices and the broader societal norms that condone and perpetuate animal suffering and environmental degradation.

For people, however, as noted in the introduction, the world is a remarkably peaceful place compared with what it was in the past. If we were visited by an advanced alien civilization, the same forces that expanded our circle would likely have taken place in their civilization as well. They would avoid annihilating us. (It turns out that *Independence Day* was unrealistic after all.)

The same is not true for an ASI, which despite possessing superintelligence in problem-solving could, in many ways, be extremely dumb. As Bostrom has argued, an ASI may decide to destroy humanity for something as trivial as building paperclips.

45

Why? Suppose that a paper clip company beats Google and the Pentagon to become the first organization to crack AGI, programming it to build as many paper clips as possible. As Bostrom argues, "The AI will realize quickly that it would be much better if there were no humans because humans might decide to switch it off. Because if humans do so, there would be fewer paper clips. Also, human bodies contain a lot of atoms that could be made into paper clips. The future that the AI would be trying to gear toward would be one in which there were a lot of paper clips but no humans."[76] Remember, it could do things as incomprehensible to humans as calculus is to mice (or me for that matter). If it wants paper clips, it will get paper clips.

Of course, rather than transforming Earth into paper clips, it could turn it into a utopia we haven't even dreamed of—opportunities and consequences. Even if the best-case scenario occurs, it will be the last significant invention humans ever create. We have one chance to get it right. This is what is called the alignment problem. Though we may try to design systems to obey our commands or have goals aligned with our own, according to Ord, "The few researchers working on such plans are finding them far more difficult than anticipated. In fact, it is they who are the leading voices of concern."[77] A lot could go wrong. Perhaps we will create an ASI to maximize human happiness and end up as brains in a jar with electrodes stimulating certain receptors. Even if the majority of investment in AI research went toward solving the alignment problem, abdicating control of our destiny is inherently risky, much like if mountain gorillas had created humans hoping that we would provide them with unlimited food and veterinary care instead of what we actually did do to gorillas.

Of course, the majority of investment *isn't* going to the alignment problem. In 2015, total corporate investment in

AI was $12.7 billion. By 2021 this figure had grown by 636 percent to $93.5 billion. And this is just corporate spending. The Pentagon invests about $1.3 billion each year in AI research and the Chinese military $1.6 billion.[78] A few companies have staff dedicated to ethical considerations, but the vast majority of AI researchers are working to build intelligence that will maximize profits and win wars. It is easy to see why so much money is being invested in AI—whatever organization cracks AGI first will essentially control the world. The problem is that they may be racing not toward a finish line but toward a cliff.

Conclusion

The opening line of this book was about opportunities and consequences in store for humanity over the coming decades. Emerging technologies such as biotech and AI offer plenty of both. If we don't proceed with caution though, the consequences may render the opportunities meaningless. The problem is that, like fossil fuels and climate change, sanity checks in the tech industry can hurt the short-term bottom line given the importance of being the first to bring a new product to market. When we have leaders viciously competing for power, money, and status, safety will fall by the wayside. Dan Hendrycks of the advocacy group Center for AI Safety says there is an argument that we can simply commit to making AIs safer, but people consistently choose power, money, or the temptation to come out ahead of the competition before safety and responsibility. If precedent serves, the companies ushering emerging technologies like AI into the world will adhere to a mantra similar to Facebook's now-infamous motto: "Move fast and break things." As noted earlier, Microsoft executive Sam Schillace's guiding philosophy is that it is an "absolutely fatal error in this moment to worry about things that can be fixed later."[79]

Yet we are approaching a point at which things may not be able to be fixed later. Leaders in industries like AI and fossil fuel are well aware of this. They also know that if things go wrong, even the world's most powerful individuals won't be safe. The fact that we keep on accelerating down the same dangerous path illustrates more than anything the urgent need for a new approach to leadership. Former First Lady Rosalynn Carter put it best when she said, "A leader takes people where they want to go. A great leader takes people where they don't necessarily want to go, but ought to be."[80]

What does this new leadership look like? That is the subject of the next chapter.

Ask Yourself

Based on their actions, have today's leaders prioritized humanity's well-being and our very survival?

CHAPTER 2

The Ten Traits of Modern Leadership

In the forthcoming book *American PTSD*, Mark Gerzon delves into the dynamics of patriarchy, illustrating it as a time-honored tactic employed to suppress dissent. He articulates how this approach demeans individuals, typically men, who oppose those in power by equating them with traditionally feminine labels, such as "pussy" or "sissy," thereby insinuating weakness.

Gerzon highlights not only the election fraud but also the dominating patriarchal strategy behind it in the following examples: the first involves President Trump pressuring Vice President Pence to contest the 2020 election outcome by calling him a "pussy." In the second scenario, Rudy Giuliani, an American politician and former Associate Attorney General of the United States calls the White House legal team "a bunch of sissies" to persuade them into endorsing a baseless conspiracy of election fraud, put together by him and John Eastman, an American lawyer and academic. This strategy, rooted in toxic masculinity, has historically been effective in perpetuating gender hierarchies, manifesting as both abusive and degrading behavior. It's a tactic that thrives not only in the corridors of business but also among the echelons of American leadership. Such practices of gender discrimination are corrosive, eroding the foundational principles of our society and significantly hindering human progress in ways that are profound and far-reaching.

How do we get ourselves out of this mess? Though the solution entails more than simply "get better leaders," never underestimate the importance of leadership.

I am a leadership consultant; this is what I focus on.

As we will see in Chapter 4, women not only make excellent leaders but are also precisely the type of leaders we need at this moment in our history. This is not simply because they lack a Y-chromosome; it is because they possess the traits we need in our leaders. This is why organizations and societies must undergo a deeper paradigm shift to make feminine traits equally valued and incentivized in leadership positions as masculine traits are. For both men and women, this doesn't mean pretending to be something they are not but rather not being afraid of being more of who they are. The current leadership advice for women "to be more like a man" is outdated and exhausting for most women and usually ends up backfiring. Embracing empathy, a willingness to listen to constructive criticism, purpose over profit, and long-term thinking should be a welcomed and a core part of their leadership style.

In this chapter we focus on the ten leadership traits that will break up the toxic masculine leadership. These are feminine leadership traits that every leader should embody, whether a head of state, CEO, or community organizer, man or woman. Based on my years of experience observing leaders, these seem to come more naturally to those without a Y-chromosome, which is why I am labeling them "feminine leadership traits." It is no coincidence, however, that they could also be called "modern leadership traits." It is time to break up the traditional leadership monopoly.

For the overwhelming majority of our history as a species, men have held a virtual monopoly on leadership. This helps explain why we tend to conflate masculine leadership qualities, such as assertiveness, competitiveness, and decisiveness, with good leadership. Though masculine—or "traditional"—leadership qualities have likely driven human progress in meaningful ways and can still be effective in achieving certain goals, they won't solve our most pressing problems. Fortunately, many leaders of both genders are starting to see the wisdom of feminine leadership, which embraces collaboration, empathy, emotional intelligence, long-term perspectives, and a holistic approach to decision-making.

As we saw in the previous chapter, the decades ahead are fraught with unprecedented dangers, mostly of our own doing. Imagine, however, if women had led us through human history and feminine leadership was also what we consider traditional leadership. Where would we find ourselves today? We will never know for certain, but there are good reasons to suspect that we wouldn't be racing recklessly toward the brink of our destruction. We can't change our past but we can change our future—it is time for humanity, the entire humanity, to create something beautiful all together.

For many, a feminine approach to leadership is synonymous with sacrificing an organization's efficiency and bottom line for the pursuit of high-minded principles. In other words, something only the most naive leaders take seriously. As we are starting to see, however, these leaders may not be so naive after all. By prioritizing the well-being and development of all team members, listening, encouraging, and empowering everyone involved, leaders in any domain can foster a positive work environment in which employees feel valued and motivated. This will pay dividends down the road. Feminine leadership also encourages a collaborative approach to decision-making, seeking input and feedback from all team members. They understand that even the "lowest-ranking," least experienced individuals can provide invaluable or overlooked insight crucial to good decision-making.

Those stuck in an outdated style of leadership may believe that a ruthless, win-at-all-cost mentality will provide a decisive advantage in outcompeting the softies who care about their employees, the well-being of society, and the environment. They also fail to see any reason to take advice from those with a lower pay grade. Overall, these leaders would likely view the traits below as naive. The truth is, however, that embracing principles outside of a short-term, win-at-all-cost mentality will provide an invaluable advantage in today's world by attracting, engaging, and retaining your employees and their talent: the greatest asset in business.

1 Start caring vs. only caring about shareholders

In business, two things matter: growth and profit. Everything else is just window dressing. If a new CEO wants to implement voluntary safety measures to protect humanity, which will also significantly cut quarterly profits, she likely wouldn't remain CEO for much longer. This explains why 68 percent of species on Earth have gone extinct within the last five decades, why each summer brings record-breaking heat waves, and why we are speeding toward a cliff as companies compete to crack AI or develop other dangerous technologies, consequences be damned.[81]

This begs the question, is capitalism the problem?

I think yes and no. Free market capitalism has lifted billions of people out of poverty, generated mind-boggling innovations, and connected nations, creating interdependence and peace. With wise leaders on the top, China and the USA are unlikely to fight a war as the two nations rely on a symbiotic relationship. Businesses can truly advance humanity and global unity. Many of them already span globally across countries, cultures, ethnic groups, and religions.

The detrimental impacts of capitalism, often attributed to its inherent nature, are not an unavoidable fate but rather the consequence of short-sighted greed and suboptimal leadership choices. Contrary to popular belief, there is no legal mandate compelling companies to prioritize shareholder profits above all else. This misconception has been challenged by the emerging global initiative the "Universal Declaration for the Rights of Mother Earth," which advocates for the inclusion of ecocide as a crime prosecutable by the International Criminal Court, alongside genocide, war crimes, and crimes against humanity.[82] This movement underscores the capacity of corporations to adopt a more holistic approach to decision-making, one that equally values the welfare of employees, communities, and the environment, not just for the ethical imperative but as a strategic alignment with the long-term viability and success of the business itself. By redefining corporate responsibility in this way, it is possible to create a framework where companies are held accountable for their impact on the planet, paving the way for a more sustainable and equitable future.

As a leadership consultant, I point out that the ruthless "making money while we can" and "consequences be damned" approach to running a business is not just immoral but also outdated. Modern, effective leaders recognize the importance of valuing "stakeholders" rather than just "shareholders."

Though these terms are sometimes used interchangeably, they're quite different. A shareholder is someone who owns stock in a company. As a shareholder, you want to get the highest financial return on your investment. That means you're probably interested in how the company performs on a high level because stock prices go up when the company does well. And when stock prices go up, you have an opportunity to sell your shares and make a profit. Today, with algorithmic trading, most shareholders own shares for mere fractions of a second. Investors, and essentially all pension-fund investors, don't care about any particular company. They care only if their total portfolio goes up or down. We need to re-evaluate this, making sure that short-term profit doesn't come at a long-term loss to society and the core fabric of life. Do we know the "net profit"?

A stakeholder, meanwhile, is someone who can impact or be impacted by a company. We usually talk about stakeholders in the context of project management, because you need to understand who's involved in your project to effectively collaborate and get work done. But stakeholders can be more than just team members who work on a project together. Stakeholders come in many different forms, from independent contributors to suppliers and distributors to company executives. And they don't have to be related to your organization either—for example, an external agency you work with might be a stakeholder in an upcoming event. Similarly, your customers can be stakeholders when their preferences directly influence your product. Effective modern leaders consider their companies' operational effect on the planet's atmosphere, water, land, and wildlife as well as on future generations. One example is Yvon Chouinard, founder of Patagonia, who made the startling statement that "Earth is now our only shareholder."[83]

Prioritizing shareholders' interests over stakeholders' interests is bad for business and the world, causing CEOs to focus on short-term gains to artificially satisfy their shareholders rather than the long-term well-being of the company and everyone it's affecting.

In the USA, publicly held companies are required by law to report quarterly to Wall Street. A study published in *The Accounting Review*, the journal of the American Accounting Association, compared the before-and-after performance of American firms when the US government changed the frequency of required financial reports. It found that shorter reporting intervals "engender managerial myopia which finds expression in a statistically and economically significant decline in investments along with a subsequent decline in operating efficiency and sales growth."[84]

In the study, companies that reported annually compared with those that reported quarterly had, on average, 10 percent greater annual sales as a percentage of assets, 3.5 percent greater annual sales growth, and 1.5 percent greater return on assets. The reason is simple: Frequent financial reporting forces executives to think short-term rather than long-term, causing them to put off long-term investments to please short-term investors. According to the study, "When new regulatory mandates forced companies to increase the frequency of their financial reporting, they reduced their annual capital investments by about 1.5 percent or 1.9 percent of their total assets, depending on how capital investments are defined. Considering that the average annual capital investments of these firms amounted to about 9 percent of assets, those were hefty cuts." By contrast, with longer financial reporting cycles, executives are more likely to make wise decisions that will improve the long-term health and viability of the company, maximizing profit long-term while increasing the likelihood of "doing the right thing."

Doing the right thing is what Paul Polman did when he took over Unilever in 2009. With Andrew Winston he co-authored the book *Net Positive: How Courageous Companies Thrive by Giving More Than They Take*, in which he describes how as the CEO of Unilever (a British/Dutch company), he informed Wall Street that Unilever would from now on report its financials yearly instead of quarterly (the EU does not require quarterly reporting), while focusing on environmental and social impact through the Unilever Sustainable Living Program.[85] During Polman's tenure up until 2019, he increased Unilever's return on investment to be superior to rivals and more than double that of the FTSE index.[86]

Behaving responsibly and intelligently like Unilever under Paul Polman's leadership is a no-brainer. It's a winner for everyone involved, just ask my colleague Hunter Lovins, author of *Natural Capitalism*[87] and *A Finer Future*.[88] The reason is very simple. If you act and behave responsibly to people and the planet, your company can cut its costs, lower its climate risks, and become more insurable and investable. In addition, as much as we are told in business to focus on the "here and now," a mindset that seeks long-term wealth generation tends to diminish the flight-or-fight instinct while revealing the humanity behind the numbers. It gives the company time to check in on the well-being and the engagement of its employees and helps establish an organization's sense of purpose. This sense of purpose is vital for the attraction, retention, and engagement of talent, which is, as mentioned, the greatest asset in business. This brings us to the next facet of modern leadership.

2 Become purpose driven vs. money driven

As companies are realizing, focusing only on profit is a surefire way to ensure employees remain disengaged and apathetic. The 1999 movie *Office Space* focuses on Peter Gibbons, a cubicle dweller at a generic software company who hates his job. After he is hypnotized, Peter becomes blissfully unconcerned about appearing productive. In one of my favorite scenes of all time, he happily provides two outside management consultants with a blunt overview of his work:

Bob Slydell: You see, what we're trying to do is get a feeling for how people spend their time at work so if you would, would you walk us through a typical day, for you?

Peter Gibbons: Well, I generally come in at least fifteen minutes late, ah, I use the side door—that way Lumbergh can't see me—after that I sorta space out for an hour.

Bob Porter: Space out?

Peter Gibbons: Yeah, I just stare at my desk, but it looks like I'm working. I do that for probably another hour after lunch too. I'd say in a given week I probably only do about fifteen minutes of real, actual, work … The thing is, Bob, it's not that I'm lazy, it's that I just don't care.

As funny as this scene is, the tragedy is that Peter represents most of the workforce. According to a recent Gallup study, only 23 percent of the global workforce were engaged in their jobs—resulting in a loss of $8.8 trillion.[89] In America, over 50 percent self-reported that they're "just showing up" and 17 percent described themselves as "actively disengaged," meaning they were *trying* to hurt their employers.[90] The lack of engagement in companies is a pandemic in itself and the number one reason I am asked to provide leadership training and executive coaching.

Disengaged workers lack a real connection to their jobs. They go through the motions. They'll likely bad-mouth managers behind their backs, gossip, spread rumors, and treat customers and clients rudely. There's little interest in participating in company events and outings. In the USA alone, disengagement costs the economy around $500 billion a year. These estimates are based on a simple calculation, namely scaling the average differences in productivity between engaged and disengaged workers. The number one focus of any manager and leader should be to create meaning for their employees.

Establishing purpose is an employee engagement driver and a win-win for all involved. Employees who feel a sense of purpose in their work tend to be happier, healthier, and more productive. Purpose-driven companies understand that they are in business for something bigger than profit, and so will their employees. It is not all about "what we do" but more so "why we do it." As Simon Sinek, author of *Start With Why*, argues, discovering the "why" of a company turns into a motivational and engagement driver because it captures the heads and hearts of employees, which has been referred to as the company's "philosophical heartbeat." When employers attract workers who share the same purpose-driven mission of a company, the result is stronger financial performance. Gallup's "Employee Engagement Report" found that engaged workforces deliver 20 percent higher productivity and 21 percent higher profitability. Providing a reason other than a paycheck for why your employees show up at work each day pays off.[91]

Young people are particularly purpose-driven. According to a LinkedIn Workplace Culture report, 9 out of 10 millennials want to work for a company whose mission and values align with theirs and are willing to consider a pay cut to do so. In addition, they are educated consumers and want their consumption to match their value. Overall, they care more than any other generation about climate and social justice.[92] There are more Greta Thunbergs out there than you think.

The good news is that being socially and environmentally conscious as a business can be a real cost saver. Companies that manage carbon emissions, helping to mitigate climate change, enjoy 18 percent higher returns on their investment than companies that fail to act, and 67 percent higher returns than companies that refuse to disclose their emissions.[93] Andrew Winston, author of *The Big Pivot*[94] and co-author of *Net Positive*,[95] advises businesses to first find their core purpose in solving global challenges and then work backward from there to drive profitability. Winston has no problem with companies making money—and lots of it—as long as they do the right thing for their employees and the planet. He knows if people and the planet are not thriving, neither will business.

Renewable energy is now the cheapest of all forms of energy, and saving money with an electric fleet is a no-brainer as the price of batteries has plummeted. In addition, according to Stanford Professor Tony Seba, autonomous electric vehicles will soon be 10 times cheaper than current private ownership of internal combustion cars.[96] In many areas of the country, including my home of Boulder, Colorado, there are free energy audits to slash energy and water waste. We also have technologies to build smarter buildings, homes, grids, cities, and food systems.

The cost of inaction is higher than action, and financial institutions are starting to demand action. Larry Fink, CEO of BlackRock, the largest asset owner in the world, is asking company leaders to provide data on carbon footprints and climate risks. According to Jigar Shah, a clean energy entrepreneur and director of the Loan Programs Office of the US Department of Energy, solving climate change is "the biggest opportunity for wealth creation in our lifetime."[97]

3 Motivate through inspiration vs. motivate through fear and other negative emotions

Anthropologists make a distinction between cultures that use guilt, shame, or fear to maintain rules, etiquette, and norms. Guilt cultures emphasize individual conscience, reinforcing feelings of guilt for bad behavior. Shame cultures accomplish this by instilling society with notions of dishonor supplemented with threats of ostracism—"Will this bring shame to my family?" These societies tend to be more violent, with honor killings and blood feuds stretching back generations. In fear cultures, control is maintained through threats of retribution for breaking rules and norms—"Will I be thrown into prison for this?" Workplace cultures take on similar dynamics (in the case of fear, replacing physical violence with threats of being fired or yelled at).

There are benefits to fear. We evolved it for a reason. In small doses, it adds a sense of urgency and energy. But as I tell my clients, *The Devil Wears Prada* approach to running a workplace is a dangerous game. As Andrew Carton, Associate Professor of Management at the Wharton School, University of Pennsylvania, observed: "Fear is a normal human emotion, and—when held in check—can sometimes be a functional or even necessary way to ensure that people do not become complacent. But when fear becomes an entrenched marker of an organization's culture, it can have toxic effects over the long run." He went on to elaborate that besides suppressing creativity, fear hinders collaboration and contributes to burnout. It often causes individuals to panic and focus so intensely on avoiding perceived threats that they miss unexpected opportunities. Employees can become so preoccupied with the fear of a specific negative outcome that they experience a kind of mental paralysis, stifling their ability to think creatively and devise innovative solutions. Perhaps most critically, fear undermines learning—a vital process for preventing the very disasters that a culture of fear is often intended to avert.[98]

Carton's colleague at Wharton, Stephanie Creary, agrees. "The problem is negative emotion often breeds other negative emotions. Fear can manifest into anxiety, depression, and hopelessness, and an environment in which these negative emotions are prevalent can become a very hard one to work in and be productive. Hope, on the other hand, can breed happiness, confidence, and all sorts of positive emotions that are much more tied to positive performance and well-being."[99]

To foster a non-guilt workplace culture, leaders need to find better ways to manage their workers. The best inspire their employees. They invest in their employees' professional growth and development. They work on creating an environment of openness where they invite everyone's input. They take the time to get to know each team member, and for team members to get to know one another. They understand the value of developing trust and respect for one another on your team and beyond. People want to work hard, not because they will be yelled at or fired if they don't, but rather because they find value in their work and admire the people in charge, willing to go above and beyond to please them. Moreover, thanks to websites like Glassdoor, employees can rate how much they like working for certain companies. Workplaces of fear can result in low ratings, making it difficult to attract new talent. Treating employees like adults also helps. Instead of implementing rigid rules and punishments, give them space to operate independently. You will be surprised by the initiative and creativity employees will show when they are allowed to become their own boss.

4 Encourage—even enforce—constructive criticism and honest feedback vs. surrounding yourself with "yes men"

In the 1990s, flying on Korean Air appeared to be a dangerous proposition. The "loss rate" for a typical airline like United was 0.27 planes for every million departures between 1988 and 1999, meaning that about one accident would occur for every four million flights. Korean Air's loss rate was 17 times higher during this same period, losing 4.79 planes for every million departures. It got so bad that the US Army, which maintains thousands of troops in South Korea, forbade its personnel from flying with the airline, while Canada considered revoking the company's overflight and landing privileges in Canadian airspace. Its atrocious safety record eventually became a source of national embarrassment. "The issue of Korean Air is not a matter of an individual company but a matter of the whole country," said Korean president, Kim Dae-Jung. "Our country's credibility is at stake."[100]

Why Korean planes kept crashing was a mystery. Unlike its hostile neighbor to the north, South Korea was a stable, prosperous democracy. Its planes and training procedures were no different from those used in other countries. In 1999, the airline finally launched a comprehensive systematic investigation to figure out what was going wrong. That was when it noticed something strange: Accidents were overwhelmingly more likely to occur when the pilots, not the copilots, were at the controls. This made no sense. It was almost like experience was a liability. Only after analyzing conversations recorded in black boxes did things start to become clear.

The problem was that the copilots were "yes men," agreeing with whatever the pilot said, never questioning their judgment. And in modern aviation, as with most pursuits in life and business, this is never a good thing. The flight deck design is intended to be operated by two people, and that operation works best when you have one person checking the other, and both people willing to participate. If you have two people operating the airplane cooperatively, you will have a safer operation than if you have a single pilot flying the plane and another person who is simply there to take over if the pilot is incapacitated. Which brings about the question, should we have "a" leader-type leadership system to start with, or would we be better off having a group of leaders, each leader equally valued in the decision-making?

The blame didn't lie with the copilots themselves but rather with Korean society as a whole. In the 1960s, Dutch psychologist Geert Hofstede developed something called the "Power Distance Index," which measures the attitudes toward hierarchy, specifically how much a particular culture values and respects authority. Hofstede asked questions like, "How frequently, in your experience, does the following problem occur: employees being afraid to express disagreement with their managers? And to what extent do the less powerful members of organizations and institutions accept and expect that power is distributed unequally?" Unsurprisingly, South Korea was the second most hierarchical society in the world.[101]

In his book *Outliers*, Malcolm Gladwell makes a compelling argument that Koreans' respect for authority was the reason behind the crashes. According to Gladwell, in Korea, "You are obliged to be deferential toward your elders and superiors in a way that would be unimaginable in the US." The problem is that "Modern airplanes are sophisticated machines designed to be piloted by a crew that works together as a team of equals, remaining unafraid to point out mistakes or disagree with a captain." A typical crash involved an initial mistake compounded by another mistake and so on until tragedy struck.[102]

Fortunately, the story has a happy ending. Korean Air eventually adopted what is known as "Crew Resource Management" training designed to teach junior crew members how to communicate clearly and assertively. This transformed the airline into one of the safest in the world with a nearly spotless safety rating.

The obvious lesson from Korean Air's turnaround is that "yes men" are dangerous, whether for safely landing a plane, running a company, or leading a nation. A less obvious but equally important lesson is that sometimes it isn't enough for leaders to simply allow constructive criticism. It is unlikely that the pilots would have responded to copilots correcting a mistake with "How dare you!" It is also unlikely that the copilots were weak-willed sycophants. They were simply doing what they had been conditioned to do since birth, behaving in a way that every polite, respectful person would. Cultural traits like this are mostly invisible, appearing as normal behavior.

It is still not enough to encourage constructive criticism; to change our ingrained habits, it needs to be reinforced and rewarded. In my leadership training, we do exactly that. The "yes man" days are over; instead we invite diversity of thoughts and opinions, while developing leaders courageous enough to embrace it. The biggest mistake a leader can make is surrounding themselves with employees providing comforting lies. It directly speaks to a leader's inflated ego and weakness.

5 Become self-confident vs. egotistical

Around the same time Korean Air's planes were crashing and burning, the nation of South Africa was on the brink of doing so as well. Both the white Afrikaners and the Black South Africans were preparing for war. Reports from the time tell of average people carrying knives and handguns in public and stashing Molotov cocktails at home. There were plenty of reasons for the Black population to despise the whites and no shortage of grievances to justify retribution, which the Afrikaners were expecting. Journalists and diplomats kept a steady eye on the country, waiting for it to explode. To everyone's surprise, it didn't.

This was largely thanks to one man, more interested in reconciliation than revenge (and as we will see later in this chapter, a more feminine rather than masculine characteristic). Few people had more reason for hating the apartheid regime than

Nelson Mandela, who had spent the last 30 years of his life confined in a prison cell. South Africa would be a very different country if he had let bitterness get the best of him. Instead, he reminded his followers, "Forgiveness liberates the soul, it removes fear. That's why it's such a powerful weapon"[103] and encouraged them to "Take your guns, your knives, and your pangas and throw them into the sea."[104]

During his presidency, Mandela's approval rating among the Black population was around 80 percent. More surprisingly, almost half of the white population approved of him, many of whom had previously considered him a terrorist. Today, Mandela is seen as one of the most important figures of the twentieth century. In November 2009, the United Nations General Assembly announced that July 18th, Mandela's birthday, is to be known as "Mandela Day," marking his contribution to world freedom. In South Africa, he is seen as the country's George Washington, Abraham Lincoln, and Martin Luther King all in one.

In 1971, about 10 years after Mandela was imprisoned, a Ugandan military officer seized power in a coup. Idi Amin wasted no time turning Uganda into a police state, murdering and imprisoning hundreds of thousands of his countrymen. He issued decrees for his every whim, such as in 1972 when he ordered the expulsion of Ugandan's Asian community, giving 80,000 people 90 days to leave the country, and gifting their land and business to his supporters.

Without experienced owners and proprietors, industries collapsed from a lack of operational expertise and maintenance. This proved disastrous for the already declining Ugandan economy. In 1979, after launching an invasion of Tanzania for reasons that still aren't entirely clear, Amin was deposed and lived the remainder of his life in exile. By the end of his rule, he had ordered the killings of an estimated 300,000–500,000 people out of a population of 12 million.

Amin is remembered today for his cruelty, buffoonery, and the fact that he dabbled in cannibalism, once saying, "I have tried human flesh and it is too salty for my taste."[105]

Be like Mandela, not Amin. The end!

But to elaborate just a bit, the two leaders could be examples of any of these 10 traits I am describing here. Reading their quotes below, however, I am always amused by their contrasting egos, which is even reflected in their names. Mandela's supporters regularly called him by his clan name, "Madiba," as a sign of respect, while Amin demanded that people refer to him by his self-bestowed title: "His Excellency, President for Life, Field Marshal Al Hajj Doctor Idi Amin Dada, VC, DSO, MC, Lord of all the Beasts of the Earth and Fishes of the Sea and Conqueror of the British Empire in Africa in General and Uganda in Particular."

Near the end of his presidency, South Africans began to worry that Mandela's departure would cause race relations in the country to regress to where they had been. Many urged him to amend the constitution allowing Mandela to run for another term. Fearing this would set a dangerous precedent, Mandela told his countrymen:

> My friends. It is your dedicated civil servants who are the engine of this country. I am more of a hood ornament.

Several decades earlier, right before he was deposed, Amin said in an interview:

> I am Uganda. There is no country without me. If I leave, Uganda would burn.

After being awarded an honorary doctorate from Harvard, Mandela stressed to the audience:

I know that through this award, you are not so much recognizing any individual achievement but are rather paying tribute to the struggles and achievements of the South African people as a whole.

Shortly after he conferred himself a doctorate of law degree from Uganda's Makerere University, Amin, who was functionally illiterate, observed:

The problem with me is that I am fifty or one hundred years ahead of my time. My speed is very fast. Some ministers have had to drop out of my government because they could not keep up.

At the unveiling of a statue in his honor, Mandela thanked the crowd but made sure to stress:

Though the statue is of one man, it should, in actual fact, symbolize all those who have resisted oppression, especially in my country.

In an interview with a British news station, Amin proclaimed:

I am the hero of Africa. I consider myself the most powerful figure in the world.

I am aware that "Be like Nelson Mandela, not Idi Amin" isn't a groundbreaking insight into effective leadership, but the stark contrast between these two illuminates just how cringe-worthy an inflated ego can be. Leaders with large egos are unable to see the world with the right mindset. Many gain success early in their careers and never recover, alienating friends because of their attitude. Simply put, nobody likes them. These people see the world through blinders that make everything about them. They fail to see the bigger picture or care for others. True success in life for them is hindered before it even begins. Ironically, a Stanford study found three times the amount of narcissism in CEOs at 18 percent compared with 5 percent in the general population.[106]

There is a thick line separating confidence and ego. "Confidence means you're secure, and egotism means you're not," says Nick Bognar, a California-based therapist. If you're truly confident, you're assured that you're a valuable person, without regard for what others think (or whether other people are better or worse than you). Egotism is the opposite because it revolves around others, and according to Bognar, is usually rooted in low self-esteem.[107]

If you think you may be inching toward egotism, start by asking yourself a few of the following questions (and be honest with yourself):

1. Do you notice yourself burning bridges with people, or that it's tough to keep up long-term relationships?

2. Do you feel superiority over other people and their stupidity?

3. Are you craving recognition and attention above all else?

4. Is it hard for you to accept responsibility for your actions, and do you frequently deflect failure onto other people?

5. Do you see success as a zero-sum game and pursue achievement and recognition above all else?

6. Are you constantly comparing yourself to others, and jealous of other people's success?

7. Are you preoccupied with status, money, and physical attractiveness (either in yourself or others, think trophy

wife/husband) rather than personality traits of kindness and compassion?

If your answer is yes to any of those questions, it's a great time to start making some changes to your thinking and actions. How? Hire a professional coach, have your coach conduct a Current State Assessment and Analysis (sometimes referred to as an Open 360), with feedback about you from the people you work with, and set up an action plan based on that feedback. Make sure to include: What would success look like for me? What will be my measures of progress? How do I hold myself accountable? By when? Halfway through the coaching engagement, usually around six months, have your coach conduct a Mid-Term State Assessment and Analysis, where your coach checks back in with the same people who gave you feedback in the beginning of your coaching engagement, to make sure you are moving the needle. Finish the work together with an End-Term Assessment and Analysis with specific focus areas to continue your work and to hold yourself accountable. Ideally there should be regular check-ins from your coach, to see what is working and what is not, to adjust accordingly. Changing your mindset, thinking, and behavior is some of the hardest but most gratifying and empowering work you can do. It takes time. Don't fear regression and make sure to celebrate progress along the way, it's a journey.

6 Value and respect societal contributions and teamwork vs. seeing yourself as "self-made"

Related to both ego and surrounding yourself with "yes men" is the conceit that you are "self-made." In the 2012 presidential election, Barack Obama ignited a firestorm when he claimed that if you were successful, somebody gave you some help at some point. Mitt Romney was quick to paint Obama as a "big government" liberal who didn't respect the role of entrepreneurs in our economy: "To say that Steve Jobs didn't build Apple, that Henry Ford didn't build Ford Motors, that Papa John didn't build Papa John Pizza ... To say something like that, it's not just foolishness. It's insulting to every entrepreneur, every innovator in America."[108]

Though Obama's choice of words may have left room for misinterpretation, he was also absolutely correct: no one is self-made. No matter how successful someone is and how little they started with, they still got plenty of help along the way. They relied on a modern healthcare system, public infrastructure helped expand their business, the education system provided competent employees, ideas, and technology that weren't their own, and countless other things allowed them to achieve their goals. "The self-made person is a myth. No successful entrepreneur or business leader is a self-made man or woman," says business coach Andy Bailey. "If you think you are, then you need to take a long, hard look in the mirror because behind your success are contributions from family, friends, teachers, mentors, and coaches. If you don't see it, then you're not looking hard enough."[109]

The notion of being "self-made" is a toxic masculine leadership trait that erodes teamwork and inflates the ego. Companies regularly grow from a garage to $100 million enterprises only to collapse because the founders are under the impression that they are "self-made" and know everything. Effective leaders recognize that ideas can come from anywhere, and they actively seek out people who can help them on their journey. They rely on their teams and show their appreciation by admitting that they don't have all the answers. They also have a deep understanding of their team's strengths and weaknesses. As Bailey observes, "One of the biggest mistakes I see business leaders make is thinking they can't learn anything from people around them. All leaders have limits, and the best ones seek others' help and opinions. They build teams of amazing people, empower them to share their ideas and make decisions, and groom them for future leadership positions." As a 2017 study found, 66 percent of employees said they would "likely leave their jobs if they didn't feel appreciated, up from 51 percent in 2012."[110] Showing gratitude will keep your team motivated and ready for the next challenge.

The self-made conceit also makes it difficult for leaders to borrow best practices and ideas from other companies. You of course don't want to steal ideas; if you are simply copying what others are doing better, you won't provide unique solutions and will quickly fall behind. Instead, borrow and modify tactics. It helps to use "business advisory groups," also called "mastermind groups," composed of professionals in businesses operating in non-competitive markets. These can provide valuable insight into the ways that others are running their companies and solving problems. If you are up against a challenge, chances are that others have been there too and you can learn from their experience and mistakes. As Bailey notes, "Business is a team sport. No great company has been built solely by the efforts of one person. The entrepreneurial spirit can take you far, but when you're running a business, you have to recognize that you will need to rely on people who may have better ideas than you. When that happens, you'll not only become a greater leader; you'll see your business and company culture grow exponentially."[111]

7 Start embracing a combination of feminine and masculine traits vs. being a "man's man"

Effective leaders integrate the best qualities traditionally associated with both genders. In Chapter 4, we will explore the concept of gender in leadership more deeply, positing that women often embody the leadership traits critically needed to avert crisis. This assertion may challenge conservatives, who often champion a return to conventional gender roles, and may also unsettle progressives, wary of claims suggesting inherent differences between genders. An insightful essay by Chelsea Conaboy in *The New York Times* challenges the notion of a "maternal instinct" as an inherent, automatic trait exclusive to women, suggesting instead that it's a societal construct reinforced by patriarchal norms to encourage women's roles as caregivers, thereby limiting their professional opportunities. Conaboy highlights, "New research on the parental brain makes clear that the idea of maternal instinct as something innate, automatic and distinctly female is a myth, one that has stuck despite the best efforts of feminists to debunk it from the moment it entered public discourse."[112]

This perspective, however, contrasts with observations across all societies and the natural world, where females often assume nurturing roles, even in leadership positions. Such behaviors are not exclusive to humans but are also prevalent among our closest relatives in the animal kingdom. Sharing 98.7 percent of our DNA with chimpanzees and bonobos, humans observe a fascinating divergence in societal structures. While humans and chimpanzees have evolved societies with a tendency toward "alpha male" dominance, bonobos have developed societies led by female coalitions, characterized by peace and cooperative care.

In societies of chimpanzees, male aggression and dominance play a significant role, with males often engaging in violent conflicts. Conversely, bonobo societies, led by groups of females, exhibit a markedly peaceful dynamic. Female bonobos nurture and protect each other, forming alliances that extend beyond their immediate groups to foster a harmonious community. This contrast underscores the potential for diverse leadership models to influence societal structures profoundly, suggesting a re-evaluation of leadership qualities in the context of gender and societal norms.

Going back to our focus on human male versus female, human males invest more time in their children than do chimpanzees and bonobos—which are essentially deadbeat dads— but being a mother is much more time-consuming. As the anthropologist Barry Hewlett observed in his study of the Aka, a nomadic people indigenous to the Democratic Republic of the Congo, fathers provided more direct care to their infants compared with other societies in the study, yet "would on average hold his infant for a total of 57 minutes while the mother would hold the infant for 490 minutes a day."[113]

Masculine and feminine qualities are, of course, influenced by societal expectations. But whether it is the Aka in the Congo or liberal yuppies in Manhattan, men and women tend to exhibit certain traits; the universality of these makes it difficult to deny that they are hard-wired into our brains.

What is important to remember is that I am not referring to individuals but personality traits that a person is more likely to display depending on their gender (Table 2.1). It's a universal truth that we embody a spectrum of these traits, and it's precisely this diversity that enriches us. The blend of these characteristics holds the key to the kind of leadership our future demands. Unfortunately, current leadership paradigms often prioritize, celebrate, and reward traits traditionally seen as masculine.

There are, of course, violent, competitive women just as there are compassionate, timid men. What I would be willing to bet though, is that had women been more prevalently

Table 2.1 Masculine versus feminine personality traits

	Masculine traits	Feminine traits
Cognition	• abstract • broadly focused • divergent • logical	• concrete • narrowly focused • convergent • intuitive
Motivation	• persistent • takes risks • proactive • short-term focus • revenge	• irresolute • avoids risks • reactive • long-term focus • reconciliation
Personality	• daring • egocentric • aggressive • insensitive • self-confident • adventurous	• cautious • empathetic • timid • sensitive • modest • responsible
Social Properties	• task oriented • wants to be respected • taciturn • tries to dominate others • fights back when criticized	• people-oriented • wants to be liked • communicative • passive • accepts criticism

(*Note*: This list is based on numerous different sources, including a study by The Attraction Lab and an article titled "Gender Issues Towards Communication Aspects on Women Leadership Styles in Construction Company."[114,115])

positioned in leadership roles in a culture celebrating feminine qualities throughout history, the annals of our past might have been considerably less marred by conflict, perhaps even steering us closer to global peace.

The repercussions of a predominantly masculine leadership model are stark, underscored by alarming statistics that highlight the impact of toxic masculinity: 90 percent of homicides globally are committed by men;[116] in the United States, a woman is subjected to domestic violence every 15 seconds, predominantly by her intimate partner; furthermore, 20 percent of women have endured sexual abuse in childhood. The economic toll of child abuse in the United States alone is estimated at $95 billion annually.[117]

These figures are a call to action, urging us to dismantle the patriarchal structures that perpetuate such cycles of violence and inequality. By embracing and valuing the full spectrum of human traits across genders, we can forge a path toward more compassionate, equitable, and effective leadership.

Non-toxic masculine traits have their benefits. With men in charge, societies tended to be more daring and audacious, taking risks and pushing boundaries. Moreover, the past was an incredibly violent place, so it made sense to look toward the most aggressive, physically strong, dominant person in the room to be the leader. As we saw in Chapter 1, however, our biggest threats are no longer barbarians at the gates but rather ourselves. Given the risks we face, we need more leaders who are responsible, compassionate, and focused on the long term, and most importantly collaborators across ethnicity groups, borders, and gender. No longer can we afford an all-boys club of leaders.

Female leaders regularly go out of their way to appear masculine. The disgraced CEO Elizabeth Holmes, who we will take a closer look at in Chapter 4, even went as far as to lower her voice. This is a misunderstanding of what female leadership is really about.

Male leaders should do more to embrace their feminine qualities. This is not a liability but rather an opportunity. I don't mean changing your voice (please don't do this) but instead showing that you are sensitive, caring, and nurturing, the qualities that people are more likely to associate with women.

Barack Obama is a good example of a leader who displayed both masculine and feminine qualities. In 2016, he wrote an article for *Glamour* describing himself as a feminist: "It's important for them [his daughters] to see role models out in the world who climb to the highest levels of whatever field they choose. And yes, it's important that their dad is a feminist because now that's what they expect of all men."[118] There are, of course, plenty of leaders who still go out of their way to appear as a "man's man" and more often than not embarrass themselves in the process.

8 Innovate, take risks, and try new things vs. sticking with what is easy and familiar

Though there is a fine line between boldness and foolishness, good leaders need to be able to step out of their comfort zone and take risks. In a study titled "Bold or Reckless? The Impact of Workplace Risk-Taking on Attributions and Expected Outcomes," researchers found that taking a risk considerably increases perceptions of a leader as energetic and proactive, traits that are passed on to their employees. They also found that taking a risk is more likely to get a person hired or promoted, which holds true even when the risks fail.[119]

Like any other leadership quality, being a good risk-taker can be a learned skill and one that requires practice. As Eleanor Roosevelt advised, "Do one thing every day that scares you."[120] Start by taking small risks that don't have serious downsides. This could be as simple as changing the brand of coffee in a break room. You can even practice taking risks in places other than work. If you are afraid of confronting others about their mistakes, practice by asking a waiter to rectify a mistake on your order. Once you become more comfortable with taking small risks, you can progress toward taking larger, more consequential risks.

When deciding whether to take a risk or try something new, it is worth considering what your motivation is. The primary difference between boldness and foolishness is the purpose. Ask yourself what you hope to accomplish and whether the risks are aligned with the goals of your team. Taking a risk for the sake of your ego is foolishness, but doing so to further the objectives of your team is boldness.

Don't disregard your initial gut feeling entirely, but be cautious of self-deception. When weighing the evidence in deciding whether or not to take a chance, realize how much wishful thinking influences us. You will likely search for evidence supporting the decision that you want to be true. This is called confirmation bias: the tendency to search for, interpret, favor, and recall information that confirms or supports one's prior beliefs or values. The internet poured gasoline on this already common human tendency.

Watch out, also, for the sunk cost fallacy when evaluating risks: the tendency to continue an endeavor once an investment in money, effort, or time has been made. This is also known as the "Concorde fallacy," referring to the UK and French governments' effort to justify their continued investment in the costly supersonic jet as a rationale for continuing the project, as opposed to realizing that it was long past time to "cut their losses."[121]

We often perceive our brain as a judge, diligently assessing evidence and leading us toward wisdom. However, as psychologist Jonathan Haidt has astutely noted, it functions more like a lawyer, adept at crafting justifications and arguments to support our desires. This "lawyer brain" is also responsible for the difficulty we face in reconsidering our beliefs, the topic of our next trait.[122]

9 Engage in debates respectfully vs. engage in arguments angrily, belittling others

In 2006 Jack Dorsey introduced Twitter to the world. And ever since, arguing with strangers on the internet has replaced baseball as America's pastime. We all know this is a pointless thing to do. Even if you're discussing something in person, people's minds are difficult to change, especially when it comes to politics. And most of us are terrible persuaders. This is creating fissures in America not seen since the Civil War.

In the past two decades, the percentage of Americans who consistently hold liberal or conservative beliefs—rather than a mix of the two—has jumped from 10 percent to over 20 percent. At the same time, beliefs about the other side are becoming more negative. Since 1994, the number of Americans who see the opposing political party as a threat to "the nation's well-being" has doubled.[123] This deepening polarization has predictable results: government shutdowns, violent protests, and scathing, and increasingly physical, attacks on elected officials. Talk of Civil War 2.0 is growing each day.

Countless studies show that throwing out facts isn't a good way to convince others that you are correct. This is because we rarely argue to learn: we compete for social status. Our minds evolved the ability to reason, not to help us find the truth but rather to help us spin arguments in our favor. As mentioned, psychologist Jonathan Haidt compares our brain to a lawyer, coming up with arguments for why it is correct, not a judge weighing evidence so "if you want to change people's minds, don't appeal to their reason. Appeal to reason's boss: the underlying moral intuitions whose conclusions reason defends."[124] If you use facts to support an argument, be sure that you also validate their morality. Then offer them a way out. Convince them that their beliefs are admirable. Don't go for a gut punch by belittling them ("I told you so"), ostracizing them ("Basket of deplorables"), or ridiculing them ("What an idiot"). These are surefire ways to make people double down on their beliefs, creating resentment and further characterizing the other side as intolerant and mean-spirited.

It is also important to realize the social consequences of changing your beliefs. "Humans are herd animals. We want to fit in, to bond with others, and to earn the respect and approval of our peers," writes James Clear in *Atomic Habits*. "Such inclinations are essential to our survival. For most of our evolutionary history, our ancestors lived in tribes. Becoming separated from the tribe—or worse, being cast out—was a death sentence."[125]

It helps to keep your arguments focused on a particular topic. Political debates often spiral out of control, starting out with something like climate change and eventually incorporating abortion, LGBTQ rights, and a myriad of other topics. Realize that it may be social suicide for a Trump supporter to suddenly become a Kamala Harris supporter and vice versa. But getting someone to be a Trump supporter who is worried about climate change or a Harris supporter in favor of gun rights allows them to remain in their tribe, possibly even making it more moderate.

My research assistant, David Lambert, helped me write this book while he was living in Ukraine. He recently told me about his experience discussing the war with people online.

Few countries have weaponized disinformation to the extent Russia has. After the war started, I wanted to do something—anything—to fight it, no matter how small. I began spending an hour or so each day debunking some of the nonsense circulating online. One of the most frustrating myths was Ukraine's supposed neo-Nazi problem, which had become a talking point in right-wing media. There is no evidence that it is worse in Ukraine than in most other European countries. In 2019, radical-right parties won about 2 percent of the vote, failing to reach the 5 percent threshold, gaining no seats in parliament. According to a comprehensive study conducted by Oxford on the radical right in the former USSR, neo-Nazis in Ukraine remain a fringe group, while in Russia, fascist philosophers like Alexander Dugin and Ivan Ilyin have been embraced and actively promoted by the Kremlin. It is a classic strategy: "Accuse the other side of that which you are guilty of."

I was upset by the number of Americans who bought into it and started commenting on posts. People would respond defensively, accusing me of being a "retard" and "shill." It was difficult staying friendly while being told that I "obviously didn't know anything about the country" by someone who had never even met a Ukrainian, using sinister-looking pictures of Zelensky, who is Jewish, juxtaposed next to Hitler as their evidence. You encounter plenty of trolls, but they quickly get bored by the polite conversation.

What truly surprised me was how many people were willing to listen. If someone commented on something I posted with pictures of neo-Nazis, I would begin by telling them that their opposition to fascism is admirable before sharing election results and academic studies. I found that sending people direct messages helped since it showed I wanted to engage in a real conversation, not a public mud fight. I would ask them if they could share any evidence that Ukraine's supposed neo-Nazi problem is worse than in other countries, trying to sound sincere. Sometimes they would point out a flawed argument on my end, and I would tell them that this was a good point and would stop using it. Eventually, most would say something like, "Look, I just don't want the US involved in any more wars." I would respond by telling them that this is a respectable point of view and one that I can respect, and how there were many, many arguments supporting their position, but neo-Nazis are not one of them.

Every so often I check their profiles and almost all of them stopped posting about Ukrainian Nazis. Did I single-handedly change the discourse surrounding the war? Of course not. But small changes can add up to big ones. I now have a pro-Putin, pro-war pen pal in Moscow whom I recently spoke with on the phone. I don't see him becoming the next Navalny, but do think I am getting through to him.

David did a lot of things right here:

- Established empathy, disarming people through kindness.

- Was respectful and showed a willingness to listen.

- Valued the other person's argument and admitted to flawed arguments.

- Indicated that he was interested in having a discussion, not a fight.

- Kept goals focused on dispelling neo-Nazi myth, not bringing in other subjects.

If you want someone to listen, you first need to listen to them. And if you want to change their mind, you need to keep an open mind yourself. Remember, politics and business aren't just about convincing other people. It's about being curious, staying open-minded, and learning. Diversity of thought is one of the most valuable commodities in leadership. This brings us to the final trait of modern leadership.

10 Be willing to change your mind when presented with evidence vs. staying imprisoned in your beliefs

Throughout our lives, one question worth constantly asking is: What have I changed my mind about recently? Learning is a lifelong pursuit, and if you still have the same beliefs that you did as a freshman in college, you're doing something wrong. One example I recently came across was Ted Cruz, whom many admire for his intellect. In a piece for *Salon*, his law school roommate and debate partner, David Panton, observed that "Ted's views today politically are almost identical to when I met him. There's nothing he says today that I didn't hear in college."[126] That assessment should be convincing enough evidence for someone staying imprisoned in his own beliefs.

With my clients, I recommend reading *The Art of Thinking Clearly* by Rolf Dobelli, which details 100 common cognitive biases that prevent us from rational thinking. Before reading it, keep in mind "blind spot bias"—the tendency to see oneself as less biased than other people, or to be able to identify more cognitive biases in others than in oneself. Some of the other most common biases include:

- Halo effect: The tendency to allow our impression of a person, company, or business in one domain to influence our overall impression of the person or entity. For example, a leader who you find attractive you may also associate with being generous, smart, and trustworthy.

- The availability heuristic: The tendency to estimate the probability of something happening based on how many examples readily come to mind. For example, after seeing several news reports of car thefts in your neighborhood, you might start to believe that such crimes are more common than they are. This is the reason why people believe the world is getting more violent when the opposite is true.

- In-group bias: How people are more likely to support or believe someone within their social group than an outsider. This bias tends to remove objectivity from any sort of selection or hiring process, as we tend to favor those we know and want to help. For example, if a male leadership group is to accept a new candidate into the group, male applicants will be preferred over female applicants. Yet another reason making it hard for women to break into upper leadership teams.

- Fundamental attribution error: The tendency to attribute someone's particular behaviors to existing, unfounded stereotypes while attributing our similar behavior to external factors. For instance, when someone on your team is late to an important meeting, you may assume that they are lazy or lacking motivation without considering internal and external factors like an illness or traffic accident that led to tardiness. However, when you are running late because of a flat tire, you expect others to attribute the error to the external factor (flat tire) rather than your behavior.[127]

These are just a few of the 100 fallacies Dobelli details. In addition to keeping blind spot bias in mind while reading this, try to think of examples from your own life, or beliefs that you hold which may be influenced by one of the biases. Knowing them can help leaders not only learn and grow but make the right decisions and realize when an argument or piece of advice is misguided, or just wishful thinking.

Conclusion

Some of these leadership traits at first glance may seem obvious. Who *doesn't* understand that appearing humble and not egotistical is a benefit for a leader? In reality, however, these fundamental traits are harder to master than we think and good leaders will constantly work on them.

I am reminded of professional athletes. I am writing this while the 2022 World Cup is taking place (inexplicably in Qatar during winter). Though I am not exactly a soccer hooligan myself, I do have children, and like most mothers I have attended my share of soccer and tennis practices over the years. While watching a news segment on the US national team, it struck me that its practice was very similar to my son's. These are professional athletes playing at the highest level of the game, yet working on the same drills as children who first stepped onto the soccer field or tennis court just weeks ago. This is because fundamentals are fundamental. Lionel Messi knows how to kick a ball and Roger Federer knows how to swing a racket, but they still spend hours a day working on it. The best leaders do the same thing. *They are lifelong learners.* These are the leaders we need. The next chapter, however, will look at the leaders we do not.

Ask Yourself

What masculine and feminine leadership traits do you lead with? Are they harmonious and effective?

CHAPTER 3

Precarious Instincts

Rise of Populism

In 2016, I watched from my home in Boulder, Colorado, as Donald Trump shocked the world by being declared President of the United States of America. It was not the only surprise 2016 offered us: nine months earlier the United Kingdom had voted to leave the EU. Right-wing populism had made its debut on two of the world's largest stages.

In Europe, support for right-wing populist parties has tripled in the past 20 years, securing the votes to place more authoritarian leaders into government posts in 11 countries. Once a marginal force accounting for only 7 percent of votes, today one in four Europeans support a populist party. In India, the world's largest democracy, Narendra Modi continues to implement a Hindu nationalist agenda. And in Brazil, Jair Bolsonaro oversaw a decades-high surge in deforestation rates of the Amazon while implementing draconian laws targeted at homosexuals. Right-wing populist leaders (RWPLs) are thriving like never before.[128] In November of 2024, Donald Trump was once again elected President of The United States of America. At the time of the election Trump was convicted of 34 felonies, facing jail time, and considered unelectable and unsuitable for Presidency by the many.

Populism—left or right—is a tricky concept to define. The *Cambridge Dictionary* defines it as:

Political ideas and activities that are intended to get the support of ordinary people by giving them what they want.[129]

This sounds like the definition of a functioning democracy. Wikipedia goes into more detail:

Populism refers to a range of political stances that emphasize the idea of "the people" and often juxtapose this group against "the elite." ... Populist parties and social movements are often led by charismatic or dominant figures who present themselves as "the voice of the people."[130]

Populism is not necessarily a bad thing. Using Wikipedia's definition, the anti-Apartheid movement in South Africa was a populist movement and Nelson Mandela the charismatic voice of the people. In that case, Mandela used his charisma to help end a racist, unjust government and emerged as perhaps the best statesman of the last century. Of course, Nazism and Hitler also fit the definition.

Populism and populist leaders can be left, right, stupid, smart, evil, benevolent, and many other things. Whatever it is, populist leaders emerge through deep feelings of discontent, not only with politics but with societal life in general.

Political scientists often point to the correlation between support for populism and economic stagnation, especially where there is economic inequality and an unwillingness or inability on the part of the government to deliver social services.

What is curious and unprecedented, however, is that even in countries where the economy is performing well—in some places, historically well—populism is thriving. In the wealthiest parts of the world, Northern Europe and North

America, right-wing populism is systematically outperform-
ing left-wing populism. Right populists tend to have larger
and more committed bases than their left-wing counterparts.
What Trump and Brexit made clear in 2016, and Trump in
2024, is that the success of right-wing movements is making
significant, real-world impacts.

Given populism's fluid definition, differentiating left and
right-wing populism is tricky. For this chapter, the important
distinction is that populists of the right generally focus on
cultural issues, and often aim to defend a national culture and
identity against perceived attacks by outsiders, whereas left-
wing populists more frequently employ economic arguments
and attack neoliberalism and the role of large corporations
in society.

Before Trump, experts and pundits told us how the
Republican Party needed to "rebrand" itself as socially liberal on most issues—especially immigration which would
welcome Latinos and other minorities—while maintaining a
fiscally conservative commitment to smaller government. In
Trump's first term, he did the opposite, and the base loved
it. It turned out that voters *did* want the government in their
lives. They wanted help. They were also angry. Trump offered
them a villain in the form of immigrant. We see similar tactics
from RWPLs around the world. At the time of this writing, is
it too early to see what Trump's second term will bring.

What is going on? A good place to start is two million
years ago.

Evolutionary Origins of RWPLs

In the early 2000s, I am embarrassed to admit watching the
entirety of a Fox reality-TV special called *Man vs. Beast*,
which pitted elite human athletes against animals, and not

just any animal but one of my absolute favorites, the great ape. Unintentionally, it taught me something.

If you Google "Sumo Wrestler, Orangutan, Tug of War," you will find a video showing a champion 363-pound sumo wrestler playing a game of tug-of-war against a 183-pound female orangutan. Within 30 seconds, the orangutan effortlessly pulled the sumo wrestler into the pit of mud that was between them. (Of course, the orangutan didn't consent to any of this and should have been in a nature reserve in Borneo instead of a TV studio.) While the human was flushed and grunting, the ape looked bored during the whole ordeal.

It is not just orangutans that make us look like wimps. Thankfully, *Man vs. Beast* didn't force a chimpanzee to arm-wrestle an NFL player, but studies show that pound for pound, our closest relative in the animal kingdom, the chimpanzee, is up to five times as strong. We do, of course, have one obvious advantage—but it comes at a cost.

The human brain is more than twice the size of an ape brain, and every gram uses an enormous number of calories. Accounting for body size, humans need 820 more calories a day than orangutans and 400 more than chimps. Not only do our brains make us weaker and slower than similar animals, but we also starve to death far quicker.

Intelligence is a powerful force but a risky evolutionary strategy. Like our distant ancestors, most people are concerned about large predators like lions. Yet thanks to the tools and technologies that our intelligence has endowed us with, they are concerned for reasons that couldn't be more different. Very few people have any legitimate reason to worry about becoming a lion's next meal, but there is a global movement of those concerned about their conservation. This is an extremely recent development.

Writer Tim Urban asks us to "imagine human history was written in a big 1,000-page book," with each page covering

250 years. If we had relied on tools and technology for survival on page one, it is unlikely the human story would have made it to page two. For the first 756 pages, we didn't even have bows and arrows. Guns don't appear until page 998.[131] For the overwhelming majority of our time on Earth, sharpened sticks were about the most powerful tools we had to defend ourselves. And if confronted by a lion, a chimpanzee—and pretty much any other wild animal in East Africa around our size—has a clear advantage. Our ability to create tools was useful, but it wasn't what allowed humans to survive and flourish. Rather, evolution provided us with an innate tool, one that was unprecedented and incredibly powerful: language.

Humans evolved in small bands of around 50–150 individuals. Other animals work together too, but our unique ability for language has no counterpart among other species. Experiments reveal that until the age of four, chimpanzees and children demonstrate the same level of intelligence. But despite many attempts to teach chimps sign language, none has acquired linguistic abilities anywhere near those human children have in their fourth year of life. Animals communicate in complex and sophisticated ways, but there is a consensus among scientists that human language is unique and unparalleled.

It was strategizing through communication and working together that made a group of humans achieve the status of apex predator. Alone, we were easy prey, so evolution hammered the group instinct into us from the start. According to evolutionary psychologist Rose McDermott, "From an evolutionary perspective, being rejected from your social group translates into a loss of resources, status, access to mates, physical protection, and ultimately survival."[132]

As humans migrated out of East Africa, our groups became larger and more varied. Today, they take many forms: nationality, ethnicity, religion, ideology, favorite sports team, and countless others. Most people have multiple groups which they take comfort in and to which they ascribe vital importance. Our instinct to form groups remains.

Rivalry between groups also comes naturally to us. There is only one other predator on this planet capable of threatening the survival of a group of 100 humans working together: a group of 150 humans working together. And this threat was not to be taken lightly. Recall from the introduction, archeological records suggest homicide rates 10,000 years ago were around 500 times higher than in today's most violent neighborhoods as various tribes engaged in near-constant warfare.[133]

Today, we have found ways to channel group rivalry instincts in nonviolent ways such as professional sports. But their far darker implications are readily apparent, from gang violence to genocides and wars.

This brings us back to RWPLs. As noted, "Populists of the right generally focus on cultural issues, claiming to defend a national culture and identity against perceived attacks by outsiders." McDermott argues that RWPLs "rely on inflammatory rhetoric to create a tribal 'us versus them' condition—this type of environment instigates neural mechanisms from the evolutionary desire to be part of the group. When the public believes there is a threat to their group, there is an instinct to become more 'groupish' and defend the group." As an example, she cites Trump's remark:

> When Mexico sends its people, they're not sending the best. They are sending people that have lots of problems and they're bringing those problems. ... They're bringing drugs, they're bringing crime. They're rapists ...[134]

There is another crucial point in understanding the appeal of RWPLs from an evolutionary standpoint: the ability to categorize things into good or bad, dangerous or safe, friend or foe, allows the cognitive efficiency to make quick and effort-less reactions. This is especially important when in danger. Rather than accepting the fact that we are in a polycrisis[135] and that the problems and threats we face are complex and difficult to comprehend let alone solve, RWPLs offer tempt-ing alternatives: immigrants are the problem, homosexuals are corrupting society, Muslims want to destroy the country. Explanations such as these are easy to understand and appear easy to solve—just build a "big beautiful wall." Of course, leaders like these are almost always wrong in identifying the problem and solution to societal issues. Scapegoating certain groups, even wealthy and powerful ones, like the much-maligned "one percent," and blaming them for all of a society's problems is, at best, ineffective. At worst, history provides a depressingly inexhaustible number of examples of what can happen when leaders who take advantage of our in-group-out-group instincts rise to power.

Misunderstanding Evolutionary Psychology

The previous section was a very brief, very simplistic over-view of RWPLs through the lens of evolutionary psychol-ogy: the study of emotions, thoughts, and behavior based on Charles Darwin's theory of evolution. I am not arguing it is the only way to explain the issue.

For a variety of reasons, evolutionary psychology is a con-troversial subject, particularly among progressives. One is that if racism, xenophobia, war, and other scourges of humanity can be explained through evolution, then it must mean they are "natural," which tacitly implies that they are okay, or even good. This is what is called the "naturalistic fallacy." British philosopher G. E. Moore coined the term in the early twenti-eth century, which is an extension of David Hume's "is-ought problem" (meaning that the way things are is not the way they "ought to be" from a moral standpoint).

There is also the notion that if something is intrinsic to human nature, then there is nothing we can do about it. The statement "War is part of human nature. There has always been war and there always will be" is an example. But as we have seen, by now war between many former enemies such as France and Germany has become subrationally unthinkable—it doesn't even come up as a coherent option, and if it ever did, would be rejected, not so much because it is unwise but because it is absurd. Just because something has always *been* part of human history doesn't mean that it always *will* be. Supporters of slavery in America circa 1860 likely said things like, "Humans practiced slavery for the entirety of history. So how could it ever change?" Slavery still exists, unfortunately, but virtually every nation has banished it to the fringes of society.

As I noted, evolutionary psychology is just one way of looking at a certain phenomenon. It is common to hear how demand for right-wing populism is high due to demographic change and advancing social progressivism. I think this is right. Other research points to misinformation, which is also probably true.

When academics or the media provide explanations for questions like "Why are RWPLs on the rise globally?" an important point is forgotten: there is never a single reason. The media loves simple narratives. Academics tend to pay lip service to the inherent complexity of such a phenomenon, but this is hastily forgotten when explaining why *their* theory is the best. In *War and Peace*, Tolstoy wrote:

When an apple has ripened and falls, why does it fall? Because of its attraction to the earth, because its stalk withers, because it is dried by the sun, because it grows heavier, because the wind shakes it, or because the boy standing below wants to eat it? Nothing is the cause. All this is only the coincidence of conditions in which all vital organic and elemental events occur.[136]

We have no difficulty acknowledging that there are countless explanations for the simplest of questions. But we forget this for things that are infinitely more complex. Debates on why racism or war exist are often like listening to one person arguing that an apple fell because of gravity and another countering that it was because of a gust of wind.

When planning this book, I didn't want it to be another liberal versus conservative polemic—we have enough of those. As you have likely guessed, I consider myself a liberal—in the way that Americans use the word. To some conservatives, this will negate anything I write. We are tribal creatures and simply don't like reading or listening to anything that suggests the opposing tribe has a point. Liberals are not immune to this, and those who think otherwise are deluding themselves. Listening to each other and working together is the only approach that has brought a better life, throughout history, and I earnestly believe that, on certain issues, a conservative approach is needed. Liberals tend to cling to the belief trans-women are indistinguishable from women and therefore should be allowed to compete in women's sports despite legitimate concerns from female athletes that being born into a "male" body still provides a decisive physical competitive advantage. The trans-issue is complex and isn't a topic I claim to know a lot about, but rather one where it appears foolish to dismiss the other side's arguments due to liberal orthodoxy. This is not just an attempt to appear bipartisan or engage in "both-sideism." There are some issues—like the fundamentals of climate change—where the debate is over. I want to emphasize, however, that this book isn't an overarching critique of all conservative beliefs. Though it goes against our natural instincts, we should always strive to "steel man" opposing viewpoints. This is the opposite of straw-manning, in which you misrepresent the other person's position or argument so you can easily defeat it. In contrast, steel-manning is when you do your best to present the most compelling version of an opposing viewpoint before making your case for why it is misguided.

To be frank, however, the men and women like the Trumps, Bolsonaros, and Le Pens of the world are the *exact* type of leaders we need to avoid at this moment in human history, considering the existential threats stated in Chapter 1. They also offer a prime example of how, especially during times of crisis and rapid change, our primitive instincts take over and suddenly "strong-alpha" leaders become more appealing. Recognizing this is an important step in creating a better future.

When researching this book, an interesting idea occurred to me: what if, in the same way that cattle begin acting agitated when arriving at a slaughterhouse, humans sense that something is wrong? It would explain why we are so anxious and pessimistic about the future. Psychologists are discovering that our actions, emotions, and motivations are driven by our subconscious to a far greater extent than previously believed.

It's probably a stretch to claim that Trumpism is a product of subconscious fears about the fate of humanity. I don't, however, think it is a stretch to claim that people sense that "as the gap between our power and our wisdom grows, our future is subject to an ever-increasing level of risk," as Ord puts it.[137] I also think that conservatives are more wary of change.

Adherents of radical right-wing ideologies might not lose sleep over the threats posed by climate change, artificial intelligence, or the risk of engineered pandemics. However, they are acutely aware of the swift transformations occurring in society, especially concerning shifts away from traditional family values, the diminishing role of Christianity, and a perceived erosion of national loyalty. For these individuals, the transition toward more inclusive family structures, the acceptance of diverse belief systems, and the concept of global citizenship represent profound sources of discomfort. Ironically, it is this very shift toward a more interconnected and inclusive worldview that is essential for safeguarding the future of humanity.

After all, a fundamental feature of conservatism is a distrust of rapid change and anything that threatens to erode the foundations of government and society, which is bad news for them since things are changing faster than we can comprehend.

As touched on in the introduction, in 2001 Ray Kurzweil published a famous essay titled "The Law of Accelerating Returns" in which he observes, "Our forebears expected the future to be pretty much like their present, which had been pretty much like their past."[138] In Tim Urban's metaphor of human history as a 1,000-page book, this was true from pages 1 to 999. Things just didn't change enough over a single generation—or dozens, for that matter—for people to notice. But look what happens on the final page of the human story (see Table 3.1).

If all these changes took place on the final page, what will the next page look like? I believe that the appeal of RWPLs is connected to the fear of a rapidly changing world. And when people are afraid, primitive instincts take over.

The problem is that sometimes what increased our distant ancestors' chances for survival now does the opposite. Much in the same way that our craving for fat and sugar—once rare luxuries in a world where one's next meal was never assured—causes numerous health problems today, our guiding instincts on leadership are putting us more, not less, at risk. There are three core leadership traits that RWPLs rely on. At this specific moment in history, these couldn't be more dangerous.

Table 3.1 The human story (*Source*: Tim Urban)[139]

Advancement	Pages 1 to 999 (250,00 years ago to the late eighteenth century)	Page 1,000 (the last 250 years)
Population	Under a billion people	8 billion people
Transportation	Walking, horses, camels, sailboats, rafts, canoes	Steamships, trains, cars, submarines, spaceships
Communications	Talking, writing letters, smoke signals	Telegraph, telephone, email, text, video calls
Mass broadcasting	Yelling loudly, books (published in print starting on p. 998)	Newspapers, radios, websites, podcasts, social media
Production	Manual tools, archaic factories	Mass production, automated machines
Plumbing	Defecating in a pot, carrying water from a well, rubbing cold water on yourself	Flushing toilets, running water, hot showers
Medicine	Herbal remedies, chisel-based surgery, magic spells	Vaccines, antibiotics, chemotherapy, advanced surgeries, personalized medicine
Energy	Pushing things with your arms, animal labor, windmills, water wheels	Fossil fuels, nuclear fission, solar, hydroelectric, wind, and other forms of renewable energies
Electricity	Non-existent	Existent
Weapons	Fists, fingernails, clubs, bows and arrows, knives, cannons, guns (p. 998)	Machine guns, tanks, missiles, drones, and—most troubling of all—nuclear, biological, and chemical weapons
Computing	Thinking, counting, abacus	Computers
Data storage	Brains, stone tablets, paper	Hard drives
Intelligence	Human	Human and artificial
Global brain	None	The internet

Three Common Traits of RWPLs

Anti-intellectualism

Inherent to any democracy is a tension between expert opinion and the desire of the public. It is the job of our leaders to find a balance between the two. To outright vilify expertise, however, is a dangerous road to take. There is a reason that some of the most dangerous, destructive regimes in history made it their foremost priority to manipulate and vilify the highly educated. Anti-intellectualism is nothing new in American politics. In 1963, historian Richard Hofstadter's published his seminal book *Anti-intellectualism in American Life*. In it, he defined anti-intellectualism as "a resentment and suspicion of the life of the mind and of those who are considered to represent it; and a disposition constantly to minimize the value of that life."[140] Today, we are seeing the acceleration of a social attitude that systematically undermines science-based facts, academic and institutional authorities, and the pursuit of theory and knowledge.

The rise of RWPLs has magnified disdain for elites and experts of all sorts, whether experts in foreign policy, economics, or even science. This is part of a larger wave of anti-rationalism that has been accelerating for years—manifested in the growing ascendance of emotion over reason in public debates, the blurring of lines among facts, opinions, and lies, as well as growing denialism in the face of scientific findings about climate change to vaccinations.

Imagine you were on a plane and the pilot fainted. You know for certain one of the other passengers happens to also be an experienced pilot. Another passenger, however, claims that he's spent hours on the internet researching how to fly a plane. A vote is taken on who should take control. If the majority vote for the guy who assures everyone he has done plenty of research on flying planes instead of the passenger with a pilot license and extensive experience, you would not only think everyone had lost their mind but also be terrified. This is not too dissimilar from what is going on now, whether in terms of climate change or public skepticism over scientific consensus of any sort.

Blaming the "out-group"

RWPLs all use the old political trick of creating a view of the world divided into "us" and "them." Trump, for example, focuses on two key messages that reinforce this division: stopping immigration from certain groups and "making America great again." His identification of immigrants as an "out-group" creates a shared identity for his followers as the "in-group." When this takes hold, politics becomes a competition between us, "the good people," versus an opposition comprised of "idiots, traitors, and criminals."

This technique has been used by people in power since time immemorial; who the bad people are changes according to the situation. Focusing on out-group threats may be an old trick but it's effective because our brains are highly sensitive to out-group attacks on in-group members. From an evolutionary perspective, out-group attacks often posed an existential threat to the in-group, which required rallying behind the in-group leader for protection. The threats we face, however, are complex, nuanced, and cannot be blamed on a single group or individual. Though companies like Exxon share plenty of blame for climate change, so do the politicians we elect and the choices we make as consumers. In other words, we all share blame.

It is sometimes difficult for us to accept this. I often think of a quote from *Game of Thrones* author George R. R. Martin regarding our urge to polarize the world between good and evil:

The battle of good and evil is a great subject for any book and certainly for a fantasy book, but I think ultimately the battle between good and evil is weighed within the individual human heart and not necessarily between an army of people dressed in white and an army of people dressed in black. When I look at the world, I see that most real living breathing human beings are grey.[141]

Isolationism

The final, and in my opinion the most dangerous, trait of RWPLs I want to note is their isolationist inclinations. As Chapter 1 made clear, we are all in this together. The most urgent issues are no longer local and national but global. This, of course, means that their solutions are too and calls for a level of global collective action never seen before. The threats we face cannot be contained by national borders any more than hurricanes can. Among RWPLs, however, there is a common philosophical thread that emphasizes isolationism—minimizing a country's involvement in international affairs, often by avoiding alliances, international laws and treaties, and interventions in foreign conflicts. The ideology is meant to prioritize solving domestic problems and putting, for example, "America first." Since President Trump took office, the United states has exited both the Paris Agreement, and the World Health Organization, and is no longer regarded as a global leader, nor a collaborator on solving our climate crisis or next global pandemic. Both are considered, as you saw in Chapter 1, to be threats to our well-being and our very survival.

As an example, once considered much more hawkish than Democrats, today's Republican Party is the primary source of opposition to providing Ukraine with crucial military assistance. Vice President Vance has stated, "I gotta be honest with you, I don't really care what happens to Ukraine one way or the other."[142] On February 19, 2025, President Trump expressed criticism of Ukraine and implied support for Putin, upending US positions on Ukraine.[143] Opinions such as these are in stark contrast to the traditional policies championed by the Republican Party. Like all global issues, "not caring" what happens to countries aside from America is not only morally wrong but also a strategic blunder. Becoming involved in foreign wars is not a decision to take lightly and more often than not, the wrong one. History has shown, however, that in some cases, ignoring or appeasing aggressive dictators just isn't an option.

Ukraine is just one example of the trend toward isolationism championed by RWPLs. Brexit offers another. Noga Levy-Rapoport, a core organizer of the UK Student Climate Network, put it best when she stated:

> We are going on strike because we are desperate to make the changes necessary for our survival. The only way we can do this is by cooperating with other countries – particularly European countries, our neighbors, friends, and allies – to legislate new, stricter regulations on the greatest polluters and contributors to global warming, namely, the oil and gas giants that operate across the continent. Leaving the EU will only exacerbate our climate problems, and Brexit is the distraction climate deniers have longed for. To allow our government to play into their hands is a betrayal of ourselves and our planet – and every young striker across the globe.
>
> The time for isolationism has passed.[144]

There is an old Chinese proverb that comes to mind. If you've heard it before, it is likely because it was used in the hit movie *Black Panther*. In the final scene, our hero, King

T'Challa of Wakanda, is giving a speech to the UN and passionately states, "In times of crisis, wise men build bridges, but fools build walls." Despite how serious our situation is, I can't help but find a bit of humor that the world's most well-known RWPL focused his campaign and now his presidency on *literally* building a wall.

Conclusion

We are entering dangerous territory, and leadership will make all the difference in the coming century. This chapter was about the wrong leaders and how our primitive instincts can lead us astray. I was wary about including it as partisanship is a dangerous element to add to any text. To some readers, this chapter will invalidate everything else this book contains. We all need to get better and recognize our tribal instincts and engage with each other on a point-by-point basis. Remember, it is easy to spot the flaws in the opposing side, recognizing the many ways in which *they* are being irrational tribalists, but few of us on either side of the political divide are cool calculators, making rational decisions based on policies. We vote based on how we feel. First, by how we feel toward the parties and their principles, and then by how we feel about the candidate. Once people have made up their minds about a party or a person, it's very hard to change their view. The challenge is recognizing *why* we feel the way we do about certain leaders and where these feelings come from, and *what* the consequences are from our behaviors and actions.

Ask Yourself

What emotions guide your preference for certain leaders and where do they come from?

CHAPTER 4

Women Leaders in a Man's World

The Gender Leadership Gap

In 2015 Elizabeth Holmes was on top of the world. Ten years earlier, when she was only 19 years old, Holmes dropped out of Stanford to found the Silicon Valley startup Theranos; it promised to revolutionize the way we diagnose illness. With a few drops of blood, Holmes claimed her product could run hundreds of medical tests, detecting conditions such as cancer and diabetes quickly and without needles or laboratories. Valued at $9 billion, the company had raised $945 million from an impressive list of investors, including media mogul Rupert Murdoch, Oracle founder Larry Ellison, Walmart's Walton family, and the billionaire family of former Secretary of Education Betsy DeVos.[145]

Much of the excitement was due to Holmes herself. Attractive with a commanding presence and distinct baritone voice, Holmes began receiving widespread praise and a litany of honors. In 2015, she was appointed a member of the Harvard Medical School Board of Fellows and was named one of *Time* magazine's 100 most influential people. Forbes ranked her as the 73rd most powerful woman in the world and awarded her its "30 Under 30 Doers Award." She was also named Woman of the Year by *Glamour*, received an Honorary Doctor of Humane Letters from Pepperdine University, and was awarded the 2015 Horatio

Alger Award of the Horatio Alger Association of Distinguished Americans, making her its youngest recipient in history. To say the least, it wasn't a bad year for her. For many, Holmes embodied the leadership potential of women in Silicon Valley.

Until it all came crashing down.

An October 2015 *Wall Street Journal* investigation found that Theranos' proprietary device could perform only about a dozen blood tests, not the hundreds it claimed. Even those demonstrated questionable accuracy. Instead, the company relied on third-party manufactured devices from traditional blood-testing companies and passed the results off as their own. Throughout her tenure as CEO, Holmes had brazenly hoodwinked investors while overseeing a company culture of secrecy and intimidation. In 2022, she was sentenced to 11 years behind bars for fraud.

Given the scarcity of female leaders in the tech industry and the intense spotlight on her even before the scandal broke, many considered Holmes, in the words of *Bloomberg* columnist Vivia Chen, "an unmitigated disaster for women."[146] Other Silicon Valley commentators like Ellen Pao have argued that it's sexist to nail Holmes for hyping her product when male tech entrepreneurs do it all the time without consequence.[147]

Regardless of how they feel about Holmes herself, something all female leaders will be able to sympathize with is the pressure on Holmes to conform to masculine notions of leadership. Journalist Lara Stemple reported:

> As a budding billionaire aiming to boost Theranos' reputation and eventual valuation, Holmes embraced all things masculine. Her black pants and turtleneck uniform were meant to conjure Silicon Valley's revolutionary, Steve Jobs ... Holmes also had a commanding presence and intensely relentless eye contact. According to some, she adopted an artificially low speaking voice. Holmes was

especially drawn to the macho world of national security, recruiting prominent statesmen and military leaders like Henry Kissinger and James Mattis to her board. She peddled the lie that Theranos tests were already in active use on the battlefields of Afghanistan.[148]

It is difficult to read this and not feel a tinge of pity for Holmes. She certainly didn't lack the intelligence and ambition to do something extraordinary. It says a lot that she felt the need to alter her voice. Though there have been plenty of influential and powerful female leaders throughout human history—Queen Elizabeth, Catherine the Great, and Cleopatra, to name a few—males have monopolized leadership for so much of our history that we automatically conflate leadership and masculine qualities.

Alice Evans, a Senior Lecturer in the Social Science of Development at King's College, London, has argued that patriarchy is as old as civilization itself. Though "there was no pre-Neolithic feminist utopia … female labor is a crucial element of the forager economy," which provided women with a more equal status during the 100,000 years that our ancestors had spent as hunter-gatherers. It wasn't until the Neolithic Revolution, when humans began to transition from a lifestyle of hunting and gathering to one of agriculture and settlement, that long-term male dominance was solidified in most societies. As Evans argues:

1. Nomadic pastoralists were especially patriarchal. Gangs of male youths banded together for external conquest. They raided communities, slaughtering local men and institutionalizing male dominance. Pastoralism spread into Europe, South Asia, the Horn of Africa, then later the Americas.

2. *Inherited wealth* was another major driver. Cattle, the plow, and irrigation raised crop yields, making land itself a valuable asset. Cereals could be traded and stored.

3. Wealth turned patrilineal *inheritance* into a key element of social organization. The more wealth a son inherited, the greater his reproductive success (by attracting wives, concubines, and rearing offspring). But this was threatened by raiders.

4. Patrilocal lineages formed to defend valuable herds and land, as well as to provide irrigation, infrastructure, insurance, healthcare, and investment.

5. To promote intergenerational cooperation, children were socialized to privilege lineage. Close-knit patrilineal kinship spawned cultures of honor.

6. Lineage cooperation, male honor, and intermarriage alliances were maintained by controlling female sexuality.

7. As societies grew they were threatened by in-fighting. Men squabbled over women, wealth, and property. Sexual jealousy was mitigated by religions that idealized sexual segregation, chastity, fidelity, and veiling. Compliance was promoted by praising female virtue, social policing, state laws, and moralizing supernatural punishment. Male rulers and theologians blamed floods, droughts, and earthquakes on disobedient women. Amid fears of eternal damnation there emerged cults of chastity. Islam became particularly patriarchal.[149]

The Dalai Lama raised an interesting point when he opined, "If we had more women leaders the world would be a more peaceful place."[150] Ironically, he is the 14th Dalai Lama in a male-only lineage. It was not until 1960 that a woman was democratically elected as a prime minister, with Sirimavo Bandaranaike of Ceylon (present-day Sri Lanka) leading her party to victory at the general election that year. By 1991, the number of countries that had some experience under female leadership reached 20. Today, 70 countries have had some sort of female leadership (elected, appointed, interim, or other), including 6 of the 10 most populous countries in the world.[151]

Despite this progress, the world still has a long way to go. Of these 70 countries, 13 had women leaders who served less than a year. Ecuador and Madagascar had women leaders for a total of just two days. In South Africa, a woman was president for 14 hours; in all three, the women were replaced by men. As of March 2021, out of 193 countries surveyed by the Council on Foreign Relations:

- 22 of the 193 (11 percent) had a female head of state.

- 13 of the 193 (7 percent) had national cabinets with at least 50 percent women.

- 3 of the 193 (1.5 percent) had national legislatures with at least 50 percent women.

- 0 of 11 (0 percent) of UN Secretary Generals have been women.

In the business world, gender inequality in leadership is even more stark:

- Women were just 8.8 percent of Fortune 500 CEOs in 2022.

- Women were only 7 percent of top executives in the Fortune 100 companies.

- Women occupy only 10 percent of top management positions in S&P 1500 companies.

- They hold just 19 percent of S&P 1500 board seats.

- They are just 26.5 percent of executive and senior officials and managers, 11 percent of top earners, and 4.8 percent of CEOs in S&P 500 companies.

- They are only 6 percent of all venture capital board representatives and lead only 9 percent of venture capital deals.

- In 2014, women were just 20 percent of executives, senior officers, and management in US high-tech industries. As recently as 2016, 43 percent of the 150 highest-earning public companies in Silicon Valley had no female executive officers.[152]

In the religious world, all religious scriptures have been written by men and interpreted by men, and all world religions developed, organized, and led by men. Religion has always

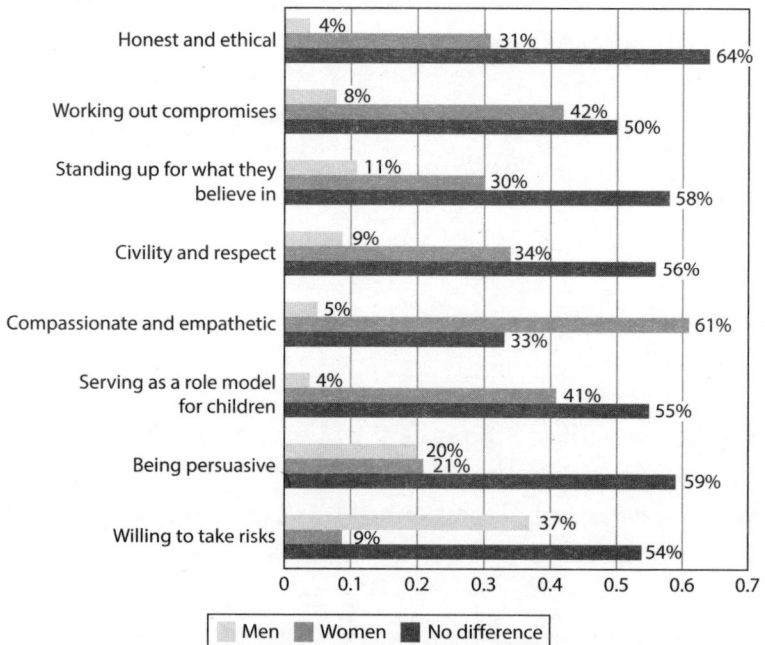

Figure 4.1 Percentage of respondents saying whether men or women are more likely to possess crucial leadership traits for high-level political positions (*Source*: Pew Research Center)[153]

been a force for men, not humanity. Countries with more religious followers and fundamentalists are also countries with fewer rights for women. Should we be surprised?

The fact that women do not dominate leadership positions is quite strange. A Pew Research Center survey asked Americans to select the most important leadership qualities for high-level political leaders and top executives. Figures 4.1 and 4.2 show them in descending order, with the most important at the top.

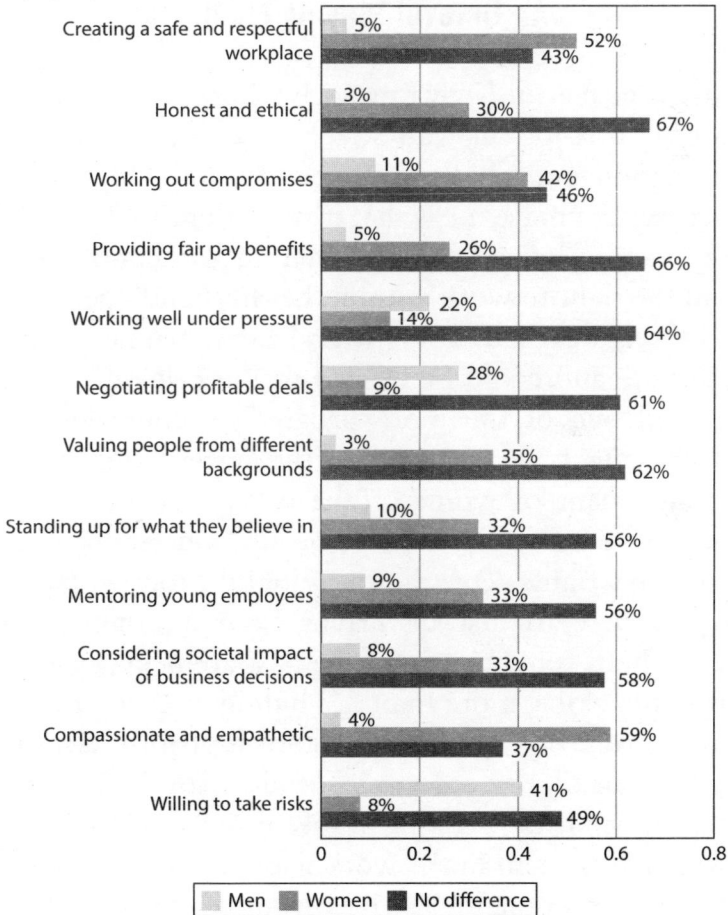

Trait	Men	Women	No difference
Creating a safe and respectful workplace	5%	52%	43%
Honest and ethical	3%	30%	67%
Working out compromises	11%	42%	46%
Providing fair pay benefits	5%	26%	66%
Working well under pressure	22%	14%	64%
Negotiating profitable deals	28%	9%	61%
Valuing people from different backgrounds	3%	35%	62%
Standing up for what they believe in	10%	32%	56%
Mentoring young employees	9%	33%	56%
Considering societal impact of business decisions	8%	33%	58%
Compassionate and empathetic	4%	59%	37%
Willing to take risks	41%	8%	49%

Figure 4.2 Percentage of respondents saying whether men or women are more likely to possess crucial leadership traits for top executives. (*Source*: Pew Research Center)[154]

Respondents were then asked whether men or women were more likely to exhibit the qualities.

Based on these figures alone, you would assume that women hold more leadership roles than men. And, of course, you would be wrong. Perhaps it is because a mere 6 percent of respondents in the same survey of 2,250 adults said that, overall, women make better political leaders than men.

An Unlevel Playing Field

Whether a farmer in Kenya or an Ivy League graduate who just got her first job on Wall Street, women continue to face discrimination and challenges men do not. One fact that never ceases to amaze me is that it wasn't until 1985 that my Swiss mother-in-law was equal to her husband under the law and had the right to work without her husband's permission. Only 14 years earlier, in 1971, had Swiss women won the right to vote and could be elected to the Federal Assembly. Considered one of the more progressive countries in the world, these facts say a lot about the current and historical disempowerment of women. Like other civil rights movements, there is still much work to be done on gender equality and women's rights. Overall, meaningful progress has been made, but there are also disturbing examples of regression, where the hard-fought gains of the past are being eroded.

Across the globe, more than 2.7 billion women are legally prevented from having the same choice of jobs as men. In 2018, 104 out of 189 economies studied still had laws preventing women from working in specific jobs, 59 had no laws on sexual harassment in the workplace, and in 18, husbands could legally prevent their wives from working.[155] Around 63 percent of women between 25 and 54 years old participated in the labor force compared with 94 percent of men, and once working, the gender wage gap was 23 percent. Even when women were participating in the workforce, they were also disproportionately responsible for unpaid and domestic work, spending around 2.5 times more time on those duties than men.[156]

In developing countries, agriculture is the most common source of work for women. Yet only 20 percent of landholders are women and their property accumulation is much smaller than that of their male counterparts. Even when governments try to push for social reforms, culture often overpowers the law. In Kenya, three-quarters of farms are run by women. Though the country amended its constitution to allow more women to own property, since 2013 less than 2 percent of title deeds issued in Kenya have gone to women.[157]

Women in these countries also face substantial inequality in health services. Surveys in low-income countries show that there are 250 million women around the globe who want to plan their families but don't have the rights, the means, or both to access contraceptives. The result: 74 million unplanned pregnancies annually.[158] Freedom to choose is a fundamental human right and one that has the added benefit of reducing pressure on natural resources.

The same is true in terms of education. Globally, there are an estimated 773 million illiterate adults, about two-thirds of whom are women.[159] The good news is that, based on UN estimates, rapid advancements in developing countries could close the education gap in 12 years if the current trajectory is maintained. The bad news is that, in some places, the trajectory is going in the wrong direction, such as Afghanistan, where the Taliban recently ordered an indefinite ban on education for girls over the age of 12 and university education for women.[160]

By increasing women's access to education, their participation in the labor force grows, population sizes stabilize, and rates of domestic violence decline. Globally, by simply having 12 years of education, on average women have four fewer children. Slowing population growth is one of the most effective strategies for curbing global carbon emissions. In the book *Drawdown: The Most Comprehensive Plan Ever Proposed to Reverse Global Warming*, Paul Hawken makes the case that educating girls and family planning rights together is the greatest weapon we have to fight climate change.[161]

Investing more in female health services and overall education is crucial for empowering women, granting them dignity, and allowing them control over their own bodies and minds. However, even in countries where women have access to these resources, the battle for bodily autonomy is far from won. In June 2021, the US Supreme Court, after nearly half a century, revoked what had been a constitutional right to abortion, delegating the authority to regulate the procedure back in the majority of states, including in the case of rape and incest in nine states.[162] This decision implied that women were deemed incapable of making critical decisions regarding their own bodies and situations by legislative bodies in 22 states. If a woman's judgement can't be trusted on abortion, how is a woman's judgement going to be trusted to lead a community, organization or nation? The court's decision suggested that these choices are better made by predominantly older, Christian, white men, effectively relegating pregnant women's bodies to state service for nine months until childbirth. One wonders how these legislators would feel if their bodies were under state control for nine months. It appears that pregnant women are not regarded as fully human with rights. Moreover, our representatives do not reflect the majority view: only 36 percent of Americans believe abortion should be illegal.[163] We need to be cautious in listening to men of "faith" in the highest positions of power. My feeling is that a blind belief in a masculine authority, "a God," can lead to an obsession about your soul's well-being and going to "heaven" at the expense of other people's suffering. Noted by Albert Einstein, "A blind belief in authority is the greatest enemy of truth."[164] I think that a preoccupation with "Jesus and God" and salvation to a "higher world" after their passing could be a threat to our entire existence.

To me, however, the Supreme Court's ruling is more about exerting control over women than upholding moral principles. Consider that a fruit fly not only has a heartbeat, but a fully functioning heart and 150,000 cells in its body, whereas a three-day-old fetus has around 10 cells.[165,166] The scrutiny even extends to the morning after pill. While I recognize that these cells hold the potential for human life, does that necessitate a moral obligation to procreate? In 2020, more than 5 million children died from preventable diseases.[167] The fact that "pro-life" advocates prioritize the unborn over children suffering and dying from preventable causes worldwide suggests that their concern is not the "sanctity of life" but control over women's bodies. This patriarchal mindset even encroaches on women's expertise, with men positioning themselves as authorities on everything from pregnancy to motherhood.

Mark Gerzon, in his forthcoming book *American PTSD*, posits that the patriarchal desire for dominance often stems from a deep-seated fear of being dominated. He argues that until we address and resolve this trauma, the cycle of patriarchy will perpetuate across generations. Perhaps the thought that every man owes his existence to a woman, his mother, is too unsettling for some. Breaking the cycle of patriarchy requires allowing women to listen to and trust their own bodies and inner wisdom.

In the business world, as we will see, the data strongly suggest women leaders tend to make a positive impact on a company, yet women still face cultural barriers preventing their rise. For a piece in *The New York Times*, journalist

Susan Chira interviewed several women who came close to becoming CEOs. Each one of her subjects cited "isolation, competition and, most chilling, deeply rooted barriers. Veiled assessments, such as lacking 'gravitas or being overly aggressive.' All comments that imply 'not like us.'"[168] This is even though these women worked for corporations that had clear policies against discrimination with male leaders who clearly stated their desire to see more women advance.

An extensive study by the *Harvard Business Review* concludes that the biases women encounter today are more harmful and destructive than the blatant discrimination of earlier decades.[169] In a study of the financial services industry, they found that women who entered the industry 30 years ago *expected* sexism in the workplace. As a result, they were more emotionally prepared for it. Now their younger millennial counterparts are shocked when they begin to encounter the unstated requirements for success in the industry. Studies also reveal that ideas of what constitutes leadership, such as ambition, assertiveness, and directness, are considered "masculine." But those same qualities in women are often perceived in a different light. If men are assertive, women are aggressive. If men are forthright and honest, women are harsh and insensitive.

On top of that, women tend to do most of the "soft work" in organizations, like planning birthday parties, buying holiday gifts, and cleaning up after events. Additionally, women tend to act as office confidantes. All of these activities— however elective—undermine women's authority and reduce the time they have to focus on career-advancing work. Amid the coronavirus pandemic, things only got worse. In today's Zoom-driven world, women are disproportionately taking on their work *plus* most of the childcare, cooking, and housework.

Women who succeed are those who can figure out how to balance the contradictions of "masculinity" and "femininity" without getting caught in a double bind. An example of a "double bind" is the woman who is labeled a "bitch" for being too aggressive but "weak" if she is too sensitive.

These are some—but by no means all—of the hurdles that women face. As we have also seen, there is a significant leadership gap between genders. Despite believing that women are more likely to demonstrate qualities that make for good leaders, the majority of people remain uncomfortable with the idea of women in leadership roles, whether in politics, religion, or business. Why? As mentioned, our perception of "who" is qualified and capable to lead has been molded by a leadership culture monopolized by men and male-centric qualities and capabilities since the beginning of human civilization 10,000 years ago. Today, we continue to associate leadership with men and masculinity, particularly in patriarchal societies like the USA.[170, 171]

The remainder of this chapter will examine what a terrible mistake this is. But first …

A Quick Reminder on Evolutionary Psychology

As touched on in Chapter 3, evolutionary psychology is a controversial subject, but also a misunderstood one that is vital for understanding human nature and therefore leadership. The left often criticizes the right for being anti-science, but progressives aren't above disregarding scientific evidence that conflicts with their political views. Sex differences are one example.

Critics from a progressive viewpoint contend that evolutionary psychology can inadvertently reinforce gender stereotypes. They argue that when certain behaviors are attributed to our evolutionary history, there's a risk of legitimizing the notion that specific actions are inherently "natural" for men or women. This, in their view, may impede the ongoing efforts to achieve gender equality and keep traditional gender roles alive. Critics are concerned that these explanations might unintentionally hinder the progress toward a more equal and inclusive society.

The progressive magazine *Current Affairs* seems to have a particular disdain for the subject, calling evolutionary psychology "the phrenology of our times," a "bullshit science" that makes "unverifiable claims" based on "scanty evidence" in order to uphold "sexist, racist, and homophobic hierarchies."[172]

To me, the existence of innate gender differences seems obvious. For anyone who has been to a frat house and a sorority, it's clear that women take better care of their environment and are less prone to physical altercations. As noted in Chapter 2, an astounding 90 percent of homicides worldwide are committed by men. Separating nurture from nature is tricky, but when the same traits distinguishing men and women consistently appear across cultures and historical eras, it becomes obvious that anatomy isn't the only difference between the sexes.

It is crucial to keep in mind, however, that evolutionary psychology is entirely irrelevant when looking at a single individual. For example, men are more likely to embrace conspiracy theories and, in the US, vote Republican. Yet Rep. Marjorie Taylor Greene built her entire career on embracing right-wing conspiracies, including the 2020 election being stolen from Donald Trump, QAnon, and Jewish space lasers. Marine Le Pen, who nearly won the French election in 2022, has stated, "The policies that I represent are the policies represented by Trump and Putin," both of whom embrace a hyper-masculine image.[173]

The point is that there are tidy pacifist men and sloppy violent women. But if you take a large enough sample size, it is clear that, no matter the culture or society, women are more likely to demonstrate certain leadership traits—which just happen to be the ones humanity desperately needs in order to survive and flourish in the decades ahead. Here are some reasons why closing the leadership gap will benefit everyone.

What Makes Women Leaders Special

Women Have a Comparative Advantage in Times of Crisis

I think it is clear to everyone by now that we live in times of crisis. As the consequences of climate change become more severe, examples of women rising to the occasion can be found worldwide. In Bangladesh, women developed wind- and flood-resistant housing foundations for their communities. In rural Sudan, women formed the first-ever women farmers union to combat food insecurity due to droughts. As hurricanes became more severe and prevalent, Nicaraguan women were motivated to create seed banks to protect biodiversity, creating sustainable livelihoods that are not dependent upon industrialized agriculture. After Hurricane Maria ravaged Puerto Rico, architect Carla Gautier partnered with her friend Maria Gabriela Velasco to rebuild 300,000 homes severely damaged by the storm. In the Pacific Islands, women have established media networks and monitoring groups to broadcast the impacts of climate change to the world. The ingenuity and strength women have demonstrated in the face of climate change have allowed communities to recover more quickly and more effectively, leading through compassion, communication, and collaboration. Perhaps most importantly, they are antidotes to despair and provide hope for the future.[174]

Covid-19 also shed light on the power of women in leadership. A study of 194 countries found that pandemic responses were systematically better in countries led by women. In the US, data also shows that Covid-19 deaths were lower in states with a female governor. During the first quarter of the pandemic, an assessment of managers in corporate America found that women leaders scored significantly higher on 13 of 19 competencies related to the pandemic response. In Figure 4.3, percentile scores for men and women are shown, sorted by the average rating for women based on data gathered in the first wave of the pandemic.[175]

Studies have revealed that women exhibit swifter inclination toward embracing innovative and preventative measures in comparison with their male counterparts. A comprehensive analysis spanning 17 international studies unveiled that women's involvement in conservation and the stewardship of natural resources yielded heightened stringency in extraction regulations, increased adherence, amplified transparency, bolstered accountability, and more effective conflict resolution mechanisms. Moreover, these investigations have shed

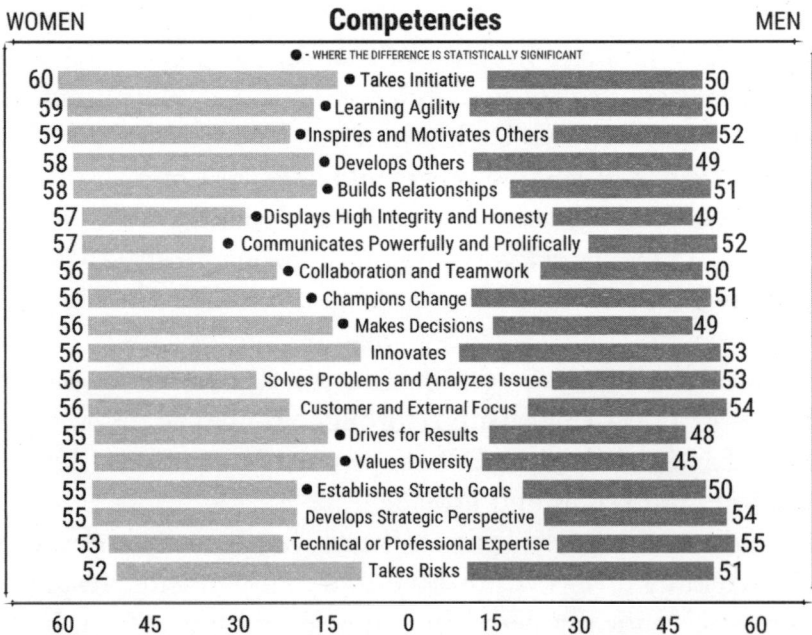

WOMEN	Competencies	MEN
	● - WHERE THE DIFFERENCE IS STATISTICALLY SIGNIFICANT	
60	● Takes Initiative	50
59	● Learning Agility	50
59	● Inspires and Motivates Others	52
58	● Develops Others	49
58	● Builds Relationships	51
57	● Displays High Integrity and Honesty	49
57	● Communicates Powerfully and Prolifically	52
56	● Collaboration and Teamwork	50
56	● Champions Change	51
56	● Makes Decisions	49
56	Innovates	53
56	Solves Problems and Analyzes Issues	53
56	Customer and External Focus	54
55	● Drives for Results	48
55	● Values Diversity	45
55	● Establishes Stretch Goals	50
55	Develops Strategic Perspective	54
53	Technical or Professional Expertise	55
52	Takes Risks	51

| 60 | 45 | 30 | 15 | 0 | 15 | 30 | 45 | 60 |

Figure 4.3 According to an analysis of 360-degree reviews during the pandemic, women were rated higher on most competencies (*Source*: Harvard Business Review)[176]

light on women's inclination for prioritizing collective welfare over individual interests. Women emerge as discernible champions of decisions that bolster the common good, foster equitable compensation and benefits, and champion honesty and ethical conduct.[177]

In the corporate world, the notion that women do well in times of crisis is no secret—and can lead to problems. There is a phenomenon known as the "glass cliff." When a company is in trouble, female leaders are often called in to save it. The problem is that a company in crisis is often already broken and the chances of anyone, male or female, saving it are slim. When women are finally given the chance to prove themselves, the odds are already stacked against them.

Women Feed the World

Women are vital for the world's supply of food. Around 70 percent of smallholder farms in Africa are managed by women, providing more than half of all nutrition to the continent.[178] (Recall how in Kenya three-quarters of farms are run by women—and less than 2 percent owned by them).

These agricultural systems have been passed down for centuries from mother to daughter, each generation adapting to changes in the land and climate. According to the UN, when women are provided with the same resources as men, they can increase agricultural yields by 20–30 percent, reducing hunger by 12–17 percent. Small-scale, women-led farms are much friendlier to the environment than industrialized agriculture, which is typically run by male-led companies and dependent upon chemical imports. Rather than expanding large-scale agricultural operations, governments could choose to support the millions of women farmers practicing regenerative agriculture, helping to close the hunger gap in their countries while preserving their environment.[179]

These lessons apply to more than agriculture. According to my colleague Hunter Lovins, president of Natural Capitalism Solutions, "Where we find ourselves today, with the state of our planet, it is not enough to be sustainable. We need to think a step further, we need to become a regenerative generation in all that we do if we are going to heal the wounds we have caused and sustain life on this planet."[180]

Much of the world depends on women for water as well. In the developing world, two-thirds of households rely on women to collect the water. Because these women hold critical knowledge of local water systems and stewardship practices, the UN has acknowledged that engaging women at all levels of decision-making and implementation is critical for sustainable water resource management. When they are excluded from the planning of water supply and sanitation projects, the rate of failure skyrockets.

Women Look After the Environment

Rachel Carson's groundbreaking book *Silent Spring* inspired a generation of grassroots action, ultimately leading to the founding of Earth Day and the creation of the US Environmental Protection Agency. Dian Fossey, Birute Galdikas, and Jane Goodall provided groundbreaking insight into the complex social dynamics of great apes and inspired a new level of public awareness about the need to protect primates and their habitats. Marine biologist, oceanographer, and explorer Sylvia Earle served as the first female chief scientist of the US National Oceanic and Atmospheric Administration (NOAA) while working to end overfishing and the destruction of our oceans. These women are influential organizers in the conservation of our planet and have inspired others to join their ranks. According to the Goldman Environmental Prize, what some call the "Nobel Prize for the environment," approximately 60 percent of the more than 200 prize winners are women.[181]

Since the turn of the millennium, women have spearheaded some of the most important environmental initiatives in the world. In 2019, an indigenous woman in Ecuador named Nemonte Nenquimo led a community action lawsuit against an oil company to prevent drilling in the Amazon. The court ruled in favor of the Waorani people, protecting half a million acres of Waorani ancestral land in the Amazon rainforest from oil drilling.[182] Kenyan activist Wangari Maathai kickstarted the Great Green Wall initiative, an African-led movement to plant an 8,000 km belt of trees across the Sahel, fighting desertification while also creating a vast carbon sink. In the USA, opposition to the Dakota Access Pipeline was led by LaDonna Brave Bull Allard, who ignited a global movement opposing its construction. In July 2020, a federal judge ruled in favor of the Standing Rock Sioux Tribe, mandating a full environmental analysis of the project. The pipeline was canceled the following year. In Honduras, a woman named Berta Cáceres waged a grassroots campaign preventing the construction of a dam on the Gualcarque River, which would have cut off water to thousands of indigenous people and destroyed their lands, by proving that it violated international treaties governing indigenous peoples' rights. These women leaders never asked "What can you do for me?"; instead they asked, "What can I do for you?" They led in service to others.[183]

It is also worth noting that without women, the Paris Agreement would not be what it is today. In 2013, a legendary group of women known as the "Lionesses" convened in the Scottish countryside and came up with the guiding principle of "net zero emissions" at a time when many parties to the climate convention were at loggerheads. The small group, which included Farhana Yamin, Christiana Figueres, and Tessa Tennant, began to grow as it incorporated female lawyers, diplomats, financiers, activists, and mothers in its mission to limit global temperature rise to 1.5°C. It was these precise targets and clear language that allowed global leaders to finally understand the urgency and, with a clear objective, begin to cooperate to create actionable policy.

Of course, on the subject of women and climate change, it is impossible not to mention my fellow Swede and Climate Hero, Greta Thunberg. At the age of only 15, Thunberg rallied the world to action through her righteous indignation and blunt speaking style. In a 2016 speech to the British parliament, she told a packed audience of MPs the truth: "This ongoing irresponsible behavior will no doubt be remembered in history as one of the greatest failures of humankind. You lied to us. You gave us false hope. You told us that the future was something to look forward to."[184]

Thunberg's message has been strikingly effective. After the speech, Environment Secretary Michael Gove provided a reply that no doubt resonated with everyone in the audience, whether they admitted it or not: "Your voice – still, calm and clear – is like the voice of our conscience. When I listened to you, I felt great admiration, but also responsibility and guilt. I am of your parents' generation, and I recognize that we haven't done nearly enough to address climate change and the broader environmental crisis that we helped to create."[185] Of course, because she has been so effective, Thunberg has predictably become a target, receiving criticism for things such as eating a banana not produced locally, having pet dogs, and using a plastic bag. Donald Trump himself felt the need to attack the teen, sarcastically stating, "She seems like a very happy young girl looking forward to a bright and wonderful future. So nice to see!"[186] The absurd, sometimes petty, sometimes cruel attacks prove one thing: the Swedish teenager is getting her message across.

When women assume managerial and decision-making roles in conservation initiatives, they consistently yield improved results. Women in leadership positions more frequently initiate and enhance climate-change policies compared with their male counterparts. Research encompassing 130 countries has revealed that nations boasting a higher representation of women in their administrative bodies are more inclined to ratify international environmental treaties. In India, a study underscored that the presence of women in leadership positions within local administrations leads to heightened rates of regeneration and canopy growth.[187] Women also serve as the custodians of native seed banks and nurseries, spearheading reforestation and conservation endeavors that mitigate forest degradation, enhance carbon sequestration, and safeguard biodiversity. Notably, the Global Landscapes Forum (GLF) recently honored 16 female leaders, including Sumarni Laman, recognized for her contributions to revitalizing Indonesia's biodiversity through a tree-planting program.[188]

In developed nations, women exhibit a greater proclivity for recycling, purchasing organic food, opting for eco-certified goods, and advocating for energy-efficient practices. European research shows that women exhibit heightened apprehension over climate change and a greater readiness to undertake sacrifices aimed at curbing carbon emissions in comparison with their male counterparts. In the US, there is a 5 percent higher likelihood that women embrace climate science.[189] As the disparity in wages and leadership opportunities between men and women closes, there exists an untapped potential to expedite the shift toward a sustainable, clean-energy economy. It is imperative that we recognize and reward the contributions of women, signaling the need to institute appropriate incentives.

It is high time for policymakers, investors, and philanthropists to recognize that when given the opportunity, women possess the potential to be a formidable catalyst for change, guiding communities, businesses, and the global arena toward a more sustainable and regenerative future. A multitude of research studies underscores the imperative need to address gender disparities in resource allocation, healthcare access, and education if we are to achieve the objectives outlined in the Paris Agreement.[190] This is the driving force behind the "SHE Changes Climate" campaign, launched in 2020, which is advocating for increased female representation in multilateral climate negotiations. Though the campaign is doing good work, the fact that it is needed at all says a lot. The climate crisis is not gender neutral and abundant female representation should have been there from the start. Women rely more on natural resources than men do. As touched on earlier, women help feed the world as agriculture continues to be a critical sector of employment for women in low- and middle-income countries. During periods of drought and unpredictable rainfall, women bear a disproportionate impact, making it harder to provide for their families. This often compels girls to leave school to assist their mothers in their struggle to provide basic needs.[191]

Fighting climate change is also a fight for climate justice, as climate change acts as a "threat multiplier," amplifying social, political, and economic tensions in fragile and conflict-affected areas. As climate change triggers conflicts worldwide, women and girls become increasingly vulnerable to various forms of gender-based violence, including conflict-related sexual violence, human trafficking, child marriage, and other violent manifestations.

When disasters strike, women are less likely to survive and more likely to suffer injuries, mainly due to longstanding gender disparities that have led to inequalities in information, mobility, decision-making, and access to resources and training. In the aftermath of such disasters, women and girls encounter greater difficulty in accessing relief and assistance, further jeopardizing their livelihoods, well-being, and recovery. This perpetuates a vicious cycle of vulnerability to future disasters. The UN estimates that of those displaced by climate change, 80 percent are women.[192]

The health of women and girls is also jeopardized by climate change and disasters, as it limits their access to services and healthcare while increasing risks related to maternal and child health. Research indicates that extreme heat amplifies the incidence of stillbirth, and climate change contributes to the spread of vector-borne illnesses such as malaria, dengue fever, and Zika virus, all of which are linked to adverse maternal and neonatal outcomes.[193]

So yes, in colossal understatement, women should be well-represented at the negotiation table, positioning them as rightful leaders in the campaign to confront the climate crisis and the manifold challenges it presents.

There is also a pressing need to provide adequate financial resources for women affected by the climate crisis and other environmental issues. In this case, "adequate" implies substantially more. Remarkably, despite the myriad of climate-related tragedies disproportionately affecting women, only 0.2 percent of philanthropic dollars allocated to environmental causes go to women's organizations, the second-to-last sector in equity rankings.[194]

What is even more remarkable, however, is that despite the outrageously low funding, female-led initiatives are making a substantial impact on a global scale. In Duncan Thomas' report "Intra-Household Resource Allocation" he noted, "In Brazil $1 in the hands of a woman has the same effect on a child's survival as $18 in the hands of a man."[195] In Guatemala, Judith Bruce and Cynthia B Lloyd found that "an additional $11.40 per month in a mother's hands would achieve the same weight gain in a young child as an additional $166 earned by the father."[196]

One example is the Women's Earth and Climate Action Network (WECAN), which has organized international events and training programs, fostering a global community of women leaders who advocate for climate justice and gender equality. Their efforts have led to the successful inclusion of gender-responsive language in climate agreements and a stronger focus on Indigenous women's roles in environmental stewardship. Another is the Global Alliance for the Future of Food. Co-led by women, the organization has advanced sustainable food systems by influencing agricultural practices and policies that mitigate climate change while ensuring food security, particularly for women farmers. By no means a comprehensive list, these accomplishments underscore the vital role that female-led organizations play in shaping inclusive, effective strategies protecting the Earth, the climate, and our future.

When Women Lead, the World Gains

Most people likely already know women care more about the environment. But what about the cutthroat world of business? What most aren't aware of is that the deficit in resources, education, and political representation women have faced for centuries has held humanity back in significant ways, preventing us from reaching our true potential—including financially.

As employment and leadership opportunities for women increase, so does the growth of companies and national economies. Businesses with three or more women in senior management simply perform better on all dimensions. In a major venture capital portfolio, companies founded by women (Theranos wasn't included) outperformed companies founded by men by 63 percent, delivering significantly higher revenue per cent. A study of over 350 startups found that women-led companies gained twice as much for every dollar invested. Data has also shown that the stock price for companies with a female CEO outperformed those with male CEOs by an average of 20 percent after two years.[197]

On the national scale, a McKinsey Global Institute (MGI) report found that if all countries in a region matched the country with the fastest-improving gender equality, as much as $12 trillion could be added to the global economy by 2025. If all women played an identical role in labor markets as men, as much as $28 trillion, or 26 percent of global annual GDP, could be added by 2025.[198]

The lack of opportunities and a myriad of challenges women face has meant generations of untapped potential and talent—potential and talent that could have led to cures for deadly diseases and solutions for global challenges like climate change. Research shows that where women have higher social and political status, their countries have 12 percent lower CO_2 emissions. We also see improvements in health and education, as well as the stabilization of population sizes, all of which are the foundations for a sustainable economy.[199]

In democracies, women tend to be more active in get-out-the-vote efforts and vote more often than men. When elected to public office, they are more likely to implement legislation protecting the environment and bolstering social welfare. In New Zealand, former Prime Minister Jacinda Ardern and her cabinet consisting of 40 percent women declared a "Climate Emergency" and set in motion a plan to make the country's public sector carbon neutral by 2025. (Jacinda Arden has unfortunately since stepped down and this goal has been moved to 2050 by current administration.) She also established a "well-being budget" in 2019 that prioritizes five key areas: mental health, child well-being, supporting the aspirations of the Māori and Pasifika populations, building a productive nation, and transforming the economy.[200] Arden, 38 years old, was only the second world leader to give birth while in office. (Benazir Bhutto, former prime minister of Pakistan, became the first when she gave birth to her daughter Bakhtawar in 1990.)

Women Create Peace

Finally, it has been shown that women are vital actors in peacemaking, and their involvement in negotiations increases the likelihood of ending violence by up to 24 percent. Given that humans are six times more likely to engage in lethal violence than the average mammal, with men nine times more likely to kill than women, this underscores the argument for more women leading humanity toward a brighter future.[201] Women have historically been the lifeblood of peace movements, as exemplified by the situation in Northern Ireland.

You might think that the largely male-dominated political sphere was responsible for ending the 30-year-long "Troubles." And to some extent, you would be correct. Out of the 110 members elected to the Northern Ireland Forum for Political Dialogue, which led to multiparty talks and the Belfast Good Friday Agreement, only 15 were women.[202] However, this view overlooks the significant, often underappreciated role women played in the peace process. Their contributions, characterized by an extraordinary blend of resilience, empathy, and a deep-seated commitment to forging a peaceful future, were pivotal in steering Northern Ireland away from the precipice of enduring conflict toward the possibility of reconciliation and harmony.

The Peace People movement, initiated in 1976 by Mairead Corrigan and Betty Williams following the tragic death of the three Maguire children, marked a watershed moment in the Troubles. The movement, emblematic of the power of women's collective action, mobilized thousands across the sectarian divide, uniting them in a common quest for peace. The leadership of mothers, symbolizing hope amid despair, illustrated the potent force of maternal grief transformed into a call for action. The global recognition of their efforts, including the Nobel Peace Prize awarded to Corrigan and Williams, underscored the significant impact of women on the peace process.

Beyond the visible spectacles of marches and rallies, women's contributions to the peace process were multifaceted and profound. In the intimate spaces of community centers, in the quiet yet fierce advocacy for cross-community dialogue, and through the relentless pursuit of justice and human rights, women were laying the essential groundwork for peace. They initiated support groups, engaged in community work, and spearheaded educational programs aimed at fostering a culture of understanding and empathy across divided communities.

The formation of the Northern Ireland Women's Coalition (NIWC) in 1996 represented a pivotal advancement in the peace process, bringing women's voices into the political sphere. The NIWC's involvement in the peace negotiations was instrumental in ensuring that the peace process was inclusive, addressing not just the political dimensions of the conflict but also its social and human aspects. The coalition's emphasis on equality, human rights, and social justice reflected the core values necessary for a sustainable peace.

At the heart of women's contributions to the peace process was the role of mothers. Their unique position—mourning the loss inflicted by the conflict while fiercely protecting the promise of future generations—imbued their calls for peace with an unmatched moral and emotional authority. Their advocacy highlighted a universal message: the cycle of violence must be broken, not just for the sake of the present but for the future of all children in Northern Ireland.

Despite the critical role women played in the peace process, their contributions have often been marginalized in the historical narrative, overshadowed by the more visible male-dominated political negotiations. This oversight fails to recognize the comprehensive nature of peacebuilding, where women's grassroots efforts and community work were as crucial as formal political agreements in laying the foundations for peace.

The impact of women on Northern Ireland's peace process is undeniable. Their actions and advocacy played a vital role in creating the social and political environment necessary for the Good Friday Agreement, marking a significant milestone in the cessation of the Troubles. The inclusive approach championed by women, emphasizing dialogue, reconciliation, and empathy, has left a lasting legacy, offering invaluable lessons on the importance of incorporating diverse perspectives in conflict resolution.

The legacy of women in the Northern Ireland peace process serves as a powerful testament to the strength inherent in compassion and the transformative potential of collective action. As Northern Ireland continues to navigate the challenges of post-conflict society, the example set by these women remains a source of inspiration and a guide for future generations. Their contributions, rooted in a profound love for their communities and an unwavering belief in the possibility of peace, have etched an indelible mark on the history of peace-building. In recognizing and honoring their role, we not only celebrate their achievements but also reinforce the critical need for inclusive, empathetic approaches to resolving conflict and building a lasting peace.

Northern Ireland represents just one of many instances where women have been at the forefront of pushing for peace amid turmoil. The sheer brutality of the civil wars that ravaged Liberia during the 1990s and into the early 2000s is difficult to comprehend. By the end, 250,000 people had lost their lives, more than one million had been displaced, and a staggering 77 percent of women had experienced some form of gender-based violence. Civilians, especially women and children, bore the brunt of the suffering.[203] Fighters with "colorful" noms de guerre like General Butt Naked—who went into battle nude—Major-General Rapist—also presumably earned for a reason—and General Mosquito Spray donned outlandish costumes such as bathrobes and pink wigs as they raped and pillaged their way through the country. Children as young as five were targeted to fill the ranks of warlords, and young men were made to consume drugs, rape women, and even kill their own family members. The title of a 2008 documentary about the role of women in ending the madness, *Pray the Devil Back to Hell*, was not an exaggeration.

In 2003, after almost 15 years of war, a group of Liberian women decided that they had had enough. In the words of their leader, Leymah Gbowee—who was awarded the 2011 Nobel Peace Prize for her efforts—the women of Liberia would "take the destiny of Liberia into their own hands." "In the past, we were silent. But after being killed, raped, dehumanized and infected with diseases, and watching our children and families destroyed, war has taught us that the future lies in saying no to violence and yes to peace! We will not relent until peace prevails!"[204] With Gbowee's leadership, the movement organized strategic tactics that would ensure the mass mobilization of women internationally to end the continuation of violence against women and famously included a sex strike. With the emphasis on religion as a non-violent framework, the movement was successful in presenting the power women as a collective hold in improving the system of injustice across nations. In 2011, Gbowee, along with two other leaders of the Women of Liberia Mass Action for Peace movement, was awarded the Nobel Peace Prize. In her speech, Gbowee reminded the world:

> There are many examples globally of such struggles by women. I believe that the prize this year not only recognizes our struggle in Liberia and Yemen. It is in recognition and honor of the struggles of grassroots women in Egypt, the Democratic Republic of Congo, Côte d'Ivoire, Tunisia, in Palestine and Israel, and in every troubled corner of the world.

One of the other recipients was a woman named Ellen Johnson Sirleaf, who in 2006 became the first female head of state in Africa. Twelve years later, after stepping down from her position of power, Sirleaf was awarded the Ibrahim Prize for Achievement in African Leadership, which recognizes "leaders who have strengthened democracy and human rights for the shared benefit of their people." In its announcement, the Ibrahim Foundation noted how, during Sirleaf's time in office, Liberia was the only country in Africa "to improve in every category and subcategory of the Ibrahim Index of African Governance."[205]

In leadership—and this is my personal opinion based on my own experience having observed and worked with both men and women in leadership for more than a decade—women tend to give more than they take. Women also tend to be more open to growth and development through coaching. In our era of leadership, all leaders need to give more than they take and instill a growth mindset, encouraging themselves and others around them to learn and grow. In today's accelerating world, American author and business consultant Ken Blanchard says it best: "No one is as smart as all of us."[206] This is similar to something called Condorcet's jury theorem, which states that the wisdom and accuracy of a group are often superior to those of a single expert. Large groups can still make mistakes, but overall, aggregated predictions of many different people will tend to do better. Leaders need to recognize this. As a leader, you need to develop a high level of self-awareness and awareness of the people around you. Because your job as a leader is to recognize and develop that talent while making this world a better place. This is why every leader needs to embrace their feminine side: to increase the well-being of themselves, their teams, and the world.

Conclusion

As we have seen, the uphill challenge women have faced is as old as civilization. This has likely held humanity back as a whole in significant ways. And for the challenges we face now and in the future, the need for women to take charge of the situation is becoming critical. It is time to end the gaps in wages, education, and leadership opportunities between men and women found around the globe in all public and private domains. Men and women alike need to speak truth to power and call for the changes needed to level the leadership playfield.

I believe that mentorship and coaching will play a key role in allowing more women to rise to leadership positions and are critical components of success. The Small Business Administration cites that 70 percent of mentored and coached businesses stay in business for more than five years.[207] Mentors have often walked the same path as their mentees. Most importantly, they open networks, which leads to opportunities that would not be available without their influence. A mentor makes a difference.

One problem for women is that leaders not only hire but also select mentees who remind them of their younger selves. If men make up the ranks of leadership, they are often mentoring other men. Seventy-eight percent of companies report that gender diversity is important in the ranks of their leadership.[208] But unconscious gender biases continue to undermine that goal at every turn. This must change if we want more women leaders. As long as women are passed over as mentees and coachees, they'll continue to languish on the lower rungs of every organization's chart. Women often don't know what they don't know. Many women are shocked to learn a male colleague or subordinate makes more money than they do. Why? Men are more willing to negotiate. And women are more likely to accept initial offers without advocating for more. Mentors can make a difference by coaching mentees through the job application and negotiation processes. Women must advocate for themselves, of course, but men in leadership roles need to make the conscious decision to understand their biases and proactively cultivate women for leadership positions through mentorships and coaching. Gender parity in the workplace will always be a pipe dream unless we complement desire with action.

Coaches are different from mentors in that they have most likely not walked in the shoes of someone they are working with, which makes them uniquely positioned to offer a "thinking outside of the box mindset." Unlike a mentor, these "off-the-beaten-path ideas" will help navigate any ingrained thinking and free the minds of the coachee. Great coaches will identify what is holding a person back and challenge outdated assumptions and beliefs while offering new perspectives. They will bring out the best in their coachees by identifying and focusing on their unique strengths while helping manage weaknesses. On an organizational level, coaches can also offer services that bring out the maximum potential of an organization, aligning values and purpose to company culture, ensuring employee engagement and overall well-being of employees.

One final—and crucial—point to note is that female and male leaders need the courage to embrace modern feminine qualities. Traditional masculine leadership qualities such as competition, the survival of the fittest, and tribal mentality, won't solve the lack of engagement in business or the existential challenges we face.

As we saw in Elizabeth Holmes, many women go out of their way to adopt masculine traits, which is no surprise: men have monopolized leadership for so much of our history that we conflate leadership and masculinity. This is outdated thinking. As noted again earlier in this chapter, women not only make excellent leaders but are also precisely the type of leaders we need at this moment in our history. This is not simply because they lack a Y-chromosome; it is because they possess the traits we need in our leaders. This is why organizations and societies must undergo a deeper paradigm shift to make feminine traits equally valued and incentivized in leadership positions as masculine traits are. For both men and women, this doesn't mean pretending to be something they are not, but rather not being afraid of being more of who they are. The current leadership advice for women "to be more like a man" is outdated and exhausting for most women and usually ends up backfiring. Embracing empathy, a willingness to listen to constructive criticism, purpose over profit, and long-term thinking should be a welcomed core part of their leadership style.

In 1984 the US government broke up AT&T in an antitrust lawsuit. Its chairman, Charles L. Brown, warned Americans that they would come to regret this, stating that he found it difficult to imagine things working as well as they had been. He was wrong. Breaking up monopolies is almost always a good thing. We didn't know it at the time, but AT&T's dominance was seriously holding back innovation. When it stopped controlling the phone lines and what you could attach to its network, many innovations started to emerge, including the answering machine and modem. The breakup of AT&T was a key step in the internet revolution. We urgently need to end the monopoly of masculinity in leadership. In order for humanity to flourish and find its full potential, it is necessary we see and value the mutually beneficial relationship between masculinity and femininity in leadership, but also in ourselves.

Ask Yourself

What do you think would be the results if a full representation of humanity led humanity in businesses, religions, and nations?

CHAPTER 5

From Classroom to Boardroom

Coincidentally, the theme of my daughter's middle school is "Leadership," yet there are concerning indications that this theme is not fully embraced in practice. A prime example is the school's approach to the cross-country team, of which my daughter is a proud member. The routine at the meets begins with both boys and girls arriving simultaneously to walk the course and warm up together. However, when the race commences, it's the boys who run first, with the girls cheering them on in front of packed stands. By the time the girls get to run, the boys have gone home and the stands are half empty. Favoring boys and their accomplishments run deep. This tradition also results in parents and female athletes spending significantly more time at these events, valuable time that could have been spent on homework and preparing for exams. A simple alternation in the running order at various meets could serve as a powerful message of equal value and respect for all students. When asked about this practice, the school's response was, "It has always been done this way." This hardly aligns with the leadership ethos the school purports to champion, nor does it foster the mindset we wish to cultivate in our future leaders.

The task of nurturing the next generation of leaders fundamentally begins with our approach to education. Over recent decades, there has been notable progress in equipping children with the skills necessary for navigating the modern world. Two centuries ago, basic literacy was a privilege enjoyed by a mere 12 percent of the world's population of secondary school age and beyond. This figure had only modestly increased by the dawn of the twentieth century. It wasn't until the 1950s that we witnessed a significant leap in global literacy rates, setting off a trajectory that would see a dramatic reversal from the statistics of 1820. Today, the scenario is flipped; where once only one in ten adults could read, now only one in ten cannot.[209] Despite these advancements, the question posed by George W. Bush, "Is our children learning", reveals a deeper concern.[210] Yes, they are learning, but are they learning the right things and are we cultivating great leaders?

This concern is echoed in the words of Italian physician and educator Maria Montessori, who is widely attributed to have remarked, "Everyone talks about peace but no one teaches peace. In this world, you are educated for competition, and competition is the beginning of every war. When he will educate himself for cooperation and to offer each other solidarity, that day he will be educating himself in peace."[211] Montessori's critique highlights a crucial flaw in our educational system: its emphasis on competition over cooperation. This ethos is palpably reflected in the dynamics of my daughter's cross-country meets, symbolizing a broader societal challenge that needs to be addressed.

Ray Kurzweil's observations on the pace of technological progress and its implications for education further complicate the picture. As we stand on the brink of a future where many of the jobs we are preparing our children for may cease to exist, the question of what skills should be prioritized in education becomes increasingly pressing. The historical context of education, from its revolutionary impact on literacy and knowledge dissemination to its current struggle with information overload, underscores the need for a paradigm shift. As Yuval Harari suggests, the focus should shift from cramming information to developing the capacity to critically navigate and synthesize this abundance of data.

The true challenge lies not in amassing knowledge but in fostering wisdom, emotional intelligence, adaptability, and mental balance. These qualities are indispensable for leadership and can, indeed, be cultivated with as much deliberacy as academic subjects. By integrating Montessori's principles of peace, cooperation, and solidarity into our educational frameworks, we can embark on a transformative journey toward developing empathetic and effective leaders for the future. This adjustment in focus from competition to collaboration not only aligns with the leadership theme of my daughter's school but also represents a vital shift necessary for the advancement of society as a whole.

What Finland Can Teach Us

The Finnish approach is an example of what education systems everywhere should look like. The country initiated over the years several novel and simple changes that have completely revolutionized its educational system. Are they cramming in dimly lit rooms on robotic schedules? No. Stressing over standardized tests enacted by the government? Nope. Finland is leading the way because of common-sense practices and a holistic teaching environment that strives for egalitarianism over excellence. The equity in the Finnish education system has led to a population equipped with strong critical thinking skills, resulting in a society bolstered by better choices of future leaders across communities, businesses, and government. As we will explore in the next chapter, there is a direct link between education and the well-being of a country. Finland has consistently ranked as one of the most socially progressive and happy countries in the world since these indexes came out. And maybe even more importantly, it can be argued that a highly educated population will stabilize democracy. Here are some reasons why Finland's education system is dominating the world.[212]

No Standardized Testing

How do we know that a student has mastered a subject, or at least demonstrates competence in that subject? The answer for much of the world is to have them fill in little bubbles on a scantron and answer pre-scanned questions. Given the immense pressure these tests put on both students and teachers, it often leads to objectives that incentivize unintended behavior that is contrary to the original goal.

An anecdote about colonial Delhi tells a story about perverse incentives. Worried that the venomous snake population was getting out of hand, the British government put a bounty on cobras, offering a reward to anyone who brought in a dead cobra. The policy appeared to be a success—that is, until the government realized that people were breeding snakes, killing them, then collecting the reward. When the governor realized that people were gaming his incentive system, he canceled the bounty. With the cobras now worthless, people released them, thus increasing the cobra population to a higher level than before the start of the program.[213]

Something similar is happening in the education system of most countries, where students learn to cram just to pass a test and teachers will teach with the sole purpose of students passing a test. Learning is an afterthought. Finland is different. The country has largely abolished standardized testing, the only exception being the National Matriculation Exam, which is a voluntary test for students at the end of upper-secondary school (equivalent to an American high school). All children in Finland are graded on an individualized basis and a grading system is set by their teacher. Tracking overall progress is done by the Ministry of Education and Culture, which samples groups across different ranges of schools.

There is, of course, a danger that a teacher may, consciously or subconsciously, show biases toward certain students and abolishing standardized testing would also get rid of a neutral way to assess a student's capabilities. This may call for a more mixed approach, in which standardized testing remains but is reformed to include emotional intelligence, creativity, and other important abilities rather than just traditional subjects. The primary point is that we need a more holistic approach in evaluating the growth and potential of each student rather than the rigid system that most countries rely on.

Teachers Are Valued

Sometimes fairly, other times not, lots of blame goes to teachers in the USA. In Finland, the bar is set so high for teachers that there is often no reason to have a rigorous "grading" system for them. Pasi Sahlberg, former director general of the Finnish Ministry of Education and Culture and the author of *Finnish Lessons: What Can the World Learn from Educational Change in Finland?*,[214] has observed, "There's no word for accountability in Finnish ... Accountability is something that is left when responsibility has been subtracted."[215] Finland's public education system views its teachers more like college professors. Each one is required to have a master's degree before entering the profession and teaching programs are the most rigorous and selective professional schools in the entire country. If a teacher isn't performing well, it's the principal's responsibility to do something about it. As writer Mike Colagrossi observes,

"The concept of the pupil–teacher dynamic that was once the master to apprentice cannot be distilled down to a few bureaucratic checks and standardized testing measures. It needs to be dealt with on an individual basis."[216]

Making the Basics a Priority

Besides being underfunded, most school systems are so concerned with increasing test scores and comprehension in math and science that they forget what constitutes a happy, harmonious, and healthy learning environment. Many years ago—42 to be exact—the Finnish school system needed some serious reforms. The program that Finland put together focused on returning to the basics. It wasn't about dominating with excellent marks or upping the ante. Instead, they looked to make the school environment a more equitable place. Since the 1980s, Finnish educators have focused on making these basics a priority:

- Education should be an instrument to balance out social inequality.

- Develop and support excellent teachers.

- All students receive free school meals.

- Ease of access to healthcare.

- Psychological counseling.

- Individualized guidance.[217]

Starting School at an Older Age and Focusing on All Students

Once again, we can see how relatively small changes can make a big difference. Finnish students start school at the age of seven and are given the freedom to simply develop without being chained to compulsory education. To put it simply, they let children be children.

A program that I am not particularly fond of is the American school program "Gifted & Talented," which selects a handful of "gifted and talented" children to nurture. Instead of searching out children who may exhibit early signs of "intelligence," we need to focus on bringing out the best in every student on a broader set of gifts and talents. In his book *Outliers*, Malcolm Gladwell observes how professional hockey players are usually born earlier compared with other children in their grade. This is because several months of development can make a big difference on the ice rink at a young age, and the fact that they are slightly older than the other children gets mistaken for athletic talent, which is then fostered by parents and coaches.[218] Parents in the USA have figured out that holding back their kids a year so they enter the school year older than most other kids provides them with the same advantages. These children are then encouraged and their talent nurtured.

If we can't recognize and nurture the potential of each child, we are at a loss. Some children are better at traditional linear thinking than others, but what I don't like seeing is children who don't possess this ability being labeled as not gifted and talented. Many of them display exactly the type of outside-the-box thinking that time and time again has proven to be extraordinarily valuable, whether in Silicon Valley, Hollywood, or the White House—the type of thinking that won't be sufficiently captured on any standardized test currently being used. Today, we need nonlinear thinkers more than ever, as climate change and other existential threats require innovative, bold solutions that nonlinear thinkers excel at creating. We have only recently begun to appreciate the fact that some children learn differently, including children with dyslexia. What worries me about programs like "Gifted & Talented" is that, like hockey players, only certain children are being encouraged and nurtured, which robs society and humanity of immense potential. We need to do a better job at unlocking humanity's true potential, not just selecting certain children who at first glance seem to demonstrate abilities beyond their peers in traditional masculine linear thinking—our world is dramatically more complex than that. To take America's school system from good to great, preparing our youth for the challenges ahead while developing our next generation of leaders, I believe all the ideas above need to be on the table.

Professional Options Other Than Traditional College Degrees

It is common these days to hear young people describe their higher education as useless. And in many cases, they are right. Children get passed on from grade to grade with the aim of getting into a good college, which is now seen as a goal within itself. Many students, however, don't need to go to college and indeed end up with little to show for the experience aside from massive debt. Finland, meanwhile, offers its young people a wider range of options for continuing their education and doesn't see such a stark dichotomy between college-educated and trade-school. Both are seen as prestigious and provide for fulfilling, financially lucrative careers. In Finland, there is the Upper Secondary School, which is a three-year program that prepares students for the Matriculation Test, which determines their acceptance into a university. This is usually based on specialties they've acquired during their time in "high school." Next, there is vocational education, which is a three-year program that trains students for various practical careers in everything from landscape design to solar installation. They have the option to take the Matriculation Test if they want to apply to university. Like all Nordic countries, university in Finland is tuition-free.

Cooperation Not Competition

Perhaps most importantly, while most Americans and other countries see the educational system as one big competition, the Finns see it differently. As writer Samuli Paronen has observed, "Real winners do not compete."[219] Contrary to most people's assumptions, this attitude has placed Finland at the top of international rankings in education. Finland's educational system doesn't worry about artificial or arbitrary merit-based systems. There are no lists of top-performing schools or teachers. It's not an environment of competition—instead, cooperation is the norm. As we discussed in Chapter 3, cooperation not competition is crucial in making it past the dangerous decades ahead. Cultivating a new generation of leaders who can see the value of working together, in combination with a population educated enough to elect those leaders, is our best hope for the future.

Finland is, of course, not the only place to look for inspiration. In Sweden, we have an educational program focused on nature offered to all children before starting school. Called Mulle, the program provides children with the chance to explore nature along with a human dressed up as a troll (Mulle) who answers questions while educating them about living in harmony alongside nature. As a child growing up in Sweden, I remember this program fondly. By connecting children with nature, they develop an emotional connection and appreciation for it and a desire to protect it. It also makes them realize that they are part of something much larger than themselves, a welcomed perspective in today's world. A simple, affordable program like this one could pay dividends in unexpected ways.

Scandinavian nations are also at the forefront of integrating empathy into their educational systems, with Denmark setting a remarkable example. Danish schools have incorporated mandatory empathy classes into their curriculum, fostering an environment where children are encouraged to openly discuss emotional challenges with their peers. Within this supportive and nonjudgmental setting, students collectively engage in finding empathetic solutions to their problems. This innovative approach to education cultivates a sense of community and understanding among students, equipping them with the emotional intelligence necessary for compassionate interaction, and prevents bullying. It is, therefore, no coincidence that Denmark consistently ranks as one of the happiest countries in the world.[220] This correlation between empathy education and national happiness highlights the profound impact that fostering emotional intelligence from a young age can have on societal well-being.

At the opposite end of the educational spectrum, in the pursuit of a sustainable future, the Eberswalde University for Sustainable Development (HNEE) is a prime example of the type of holistic thinking we need. Established in 1830 as the Higher Institute of Forestry, the university, situated just outside Berlin, has evolved into a dynamic hub for education and research, emphasizing forward-looking industries and pivotal sectors like nature protection, forest management, organic farming, climate change adaptation, sustainable economics, timber construction, and tourism management.

Comprising around 2,300 students from over 60 nations and more than 400 dedicated employees, the HNEE is on a mission to lead the transformation toward a sustainable society. The institution's commitment is evident in its 20 innovative study programs, some of which are unparalleled in Germany, spanning four faculties: Forest and Environment, Landscape Management and Nature Conservation, Wood Engineering, and Sustainable Business. This commitment extends beyond academia, as the HNEE consistently practices sustainability in all facets of its operations—teaching, research, business, and transfer—utilizing participatory approaches to continually refine its methods. Overall, programs such as this provide hope for the future and I would be thrilled to see the model spread. Going forward, all programs and degrees from all universities worldwide should be taught through the lens of sustainability.

Parental Leave—Letting Kids Be Kids

In envisioning a society that prioritizes the well-being of children, the Nordic countries serve as a compelling model, particularly in their approach to parental leave. In Sweden, for instance, parents enjoy a generous 480 days (approximately 16 months) of parental leave per child, with a guaranteed government payout of 80 percent of their current salary for 390 days, with employers often matching the rest.[221] This not only fosters a nurturing environment for children but also addresses gender imbalances in professional development and career opportunities. The Nordic countries have set up a society of *caring* through universal healthcare, child care, elder care and, as mentioned, parental leave.

The benefits extend beyond the family unit to positively impact businesses and society as a whole. By providing equal opportunities for both parents to engage in caregiving, it levels the playing field between men and women's talent in the workplace, dismantling traditional patriarchal structures. Caregiving and nurturing of another human being 24/7 offer the most essential skill in leadership, an invaluable human skill that you will not learn in leadership training or a leadership retreat. The Swedish government and business industry have understood this. This shift is also evident in Sweden's business landscape, where a more inclusive approach to leadership and management prevails, fostering innovation and adaptability. The result is a country with one of the highest number of startups per capita globally.

Scandinavian and Nordic countries consistently outperform the rest of the world in various indices of success and well-being, such as the Social Progress Index and the World Happiness Index, which will be looked at more closely in the next chapter.

Embracing a culture that values the well-being of children and its people, ensures gender equality, and supports work–life balance contributes to a more harmonious and empowered society. Such an approach not only narrows the gender pay gap, it also diminishes income inequalities between different professions. In contrast to a more masculine societal structure, where CEOs earn exorbitant salaries often up to 200 times the average worker's, a feminine society emphasizes caring professions, recognizing the importance of nurturing roles in building a compassionate community.[222]

As we reflect on these societal models, it prompts us to consider the kinds of incentives we want to promote—whether it's fostering a culture of care and equal opportunities or perpetuating a system where a few individuals amass vast wealth at the expense of the broader community. Creating a world where businesses, communities, and nations prioritize the well-being of all, rather than being driven by a select few, is crucial for a brighter and more equitable future.

Providing Equal Advantage

One final point to touch on is how many missed opportunities humanity has likely suffered because of disparities in education between the rich and poor, or male and female.

A girl from Burundi, the poorest country in the world, has the same intellectual potential as a boy from Palo Alto, California, but not the same opportunities. Collectively, this is putting humanity at a serious disadvantage. In 2023 there were 258 million children not in school.[223] Among them were likely Newtons and Einsteins who, rather than revolutionizing the world, will be plowing fields simply because they never had the opportunity to utilize their talents.

Even for children in poor countries lucky enough to attend school, the lack of resources allowing them to attend a university or start a business means that many still end up working jobs that in no way allow them to fulfill their potential. For global businesses, closing the gap in education and opportunities means a smarter workforce abroad. It is a win-win situation and we should be doing everything we can to ensure that any future Fortune 500 CEOs, scientific geniuses, or political leaders have their talents fostered and are given opportunities to utilize them when they grow older, if they so choose.

And of course, as touched on in the last chapter, boys are far more likely to receive an education than girls are. Of the 258 million not in school, 70 percent were girls. And as we saw in the last chapter, this doesn't bode well for the future.

Conclusion

As I have stressed, true leaders are life-long learners—so don't assume these lessons apply to just children. Recognizing and fostering each individual's unique strengths, values, and purpose would improve not only the education system. Much of my work relates to helping organizations and leaders identify these same things. This approach is grounded on my collaboration with Barry Conchie, co-author of *Strengths Based Leadership*.[224] The book is based on a landmark study of great leaders, teams, and the reasons why people follow them.

A strengths-based organization aims to create an employee-centric culture where individual differences are applied to make their teams and overall organization more productive. These foster a workplace culture in which an employee's specific strengths are closely examined so they can be placed in a role best suited to them. Management guru Jim Collins argues that "putting the right people in the right seat on the bus" is key to a company's success.[225] Strengths-based organizations have six times the engagement of non-strengths-based organizations. In addition, exploring, identifying, and creating an organization's "raison d'être" is truly transformational. But how do we grow as people and organizations to become life-long learners in an ever-changing environment? My advice is the oldest in the world: "Know thyself." What most people don't appreciate is how difficult this truly is. Please look at the Appendix for resources to help get you started.

Ask Yourself

Do I know my core values, my purpose, and what unique strengths I bring to this world and how I want to use them?

CHAPTER 6

Re-Evaluating Success

Gross domestic product is the market value of goods and services produced in a country over a specific period and has long been the indicator of progress and success. In post-war Europe and America, GDP growth became synonymous with improved living standards and continues to act as a lodestar guiding most policy decisions as well as a scorecard for judging the effectiveness of leaders. Like the example in the previous chapter of the people breeding cobras, we need to take a closer look at whether using GDP as an incentive is leading us to an oasis of well-being or further into the desert in chase of a mirage.

GDP emerged amid the Great Depression after Congress commissioned economist Simon Kuznets to create a system that accounted for what was happening in the nation's economy. Kuznets himself rejected the idea that the system could gauge well-being, writing in 1934, "The welfare of a nation can scarcely be inferred from a measurement of national income."[226] He understood that though his new measure captured economic activity, it had no way of determining whether that activity was good or bad for society. The BP oil rig explosion in 2014, for example, killed 11 people and devastated the marine ecosystem of the Gulf of Mexico, but it also boosted GDP given the costly clean-up effort.[227] To summarize, the bigger the spill, the bigger the GDP.

The use of GDP spread globally after the Bretton Woods Conference in 1944, which led to the creation of the World Bank and the International Monetary Fund. Both institutions adopted GDP methodologies from the USA and the UK to guide policy-making on international monetary exchanges and determine which global development projects merited funding. Today, as the European Environment Agency puts it, "Worldwide, the legitimacy of governments cannot be separated from their ability to deliver economic growth and provide employment."[228]

Kuznets was also quick to point out that GDP fails to distinguish "between quantity and quality of growth, between costs and returns, and between the short and long run."[229] It takes no consideration of the management of limited natural resources, nor the cost of this consumption to society and the effect it will have on the well-being of humans, animals, and our planet. As reflected in Figure 6.1, GDP is closely linked to increases in production, consumption, and resource use.

Because of the consumption and production of more and more stuff:

- Resource extraction has more than tripled since 1970, including a fivefold increase in the use of nonmetallic minerals and a 45 percent increase in fossil fuel use.

- Plastic pollution in our oceans has increased tenfold since 1980.

- Up to 400 million tons of heavy metals, solvents, toxic sludge, and other industrial wastes enter the world's waters every year.

- 10 million hectares of forest—about 10,000 square kilometers, roughly the size of Iceland—are cut down every single year.[230]

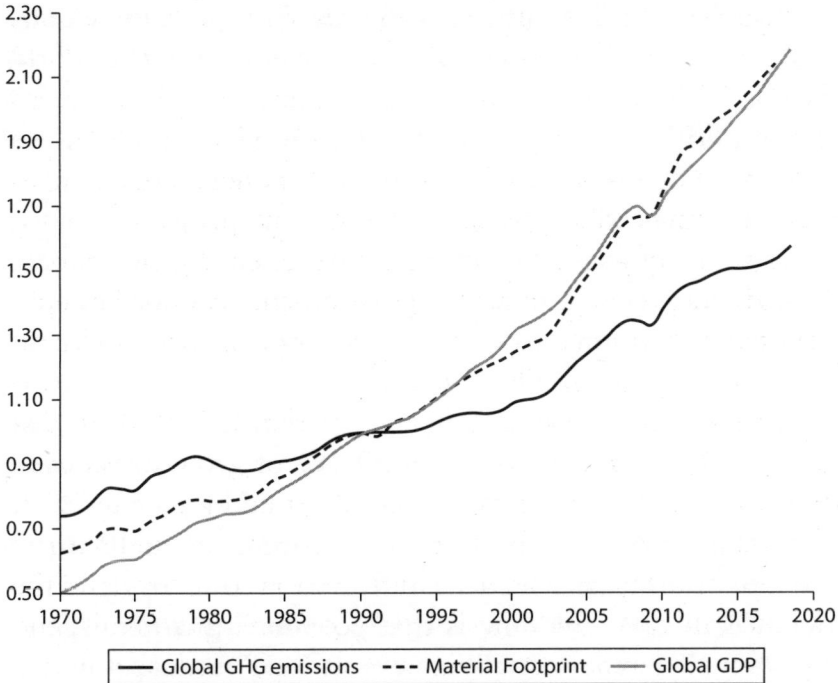

Figure 6.1 Higher GDP correlates closely with increases in production, consumption, and resource use[231]

The problem is that we cannot have continued exponential growth on a planet with limited natural resources. This is Economics 101. Earth Overshoot Day occurs each year when humanity uses all the biological resources for the year that can be regenerated in one year. In 1970, it took place on December 30—in 2022, July 28. The great irony of it all is that if stuff is your thing, you will never have enough. Dave Ramsey puts it best, "We buy things we don't need with money we don't have to impress people we don't like."[232] Yet, the latest and greatest trend in the professional world is the desire to become an "influencer," where you receive free stuff to get your followers to buy more and more stuff. Have we become that superficial?

High-level policy initiatives like the European Green Deal and the United Nations Sustainable Development Goals (SDGs) have proposed decoupling economic growth and consumption as a solution. Debates on whether this is even possible, however, stretch back to the nineteenth century, and there is still no consensus.

The current trajectory of human development is not pretty. A linear, fossil-fuel-based model of economic growth that relies on unsustainable levels of consumption and production is destroying the ecological building blocks on which our collective well-being and life depend. According to Alexander MacDonald, former director at NOAA and author of *Saving Paradise*, soon to be released, we will hit 500 ppm (particles per million) of carbon in the atmosphere by 2040 on the current trajectory, which he refers to as the "death zone." What is most frightening is that economic growth is generally modeled exponentially: our economic output grows by a set percentage every year, and while that percentage varies, it also compounds on itself.

One can't help but see our current economic system as a drug addict needing a progressively larger fix to maintain the good times. Kate Raworth, author of *Doughnut Economics: Seven Ways to Think Like a 21st-Century Economist*, prefers a different analogy, writing, "We love to see our kids grow, we love to see our gardens grow, growth is good. Growth is indeed a wonderful, healthy sign of life. But nothing in nature succeeds by growing forever...When things continue to grow unchecked, we recognize it as a cancer that will ultimately destroy the host."[233]

Some optimists have faith that technology and "human ingenuity" will save the Earth, arguing that new technology will allow humanity to continue its progress indefinitely by enabling economic growth with a shrinking environmental impact. This is what Steven D. Levitt and Stephen J. Dubner argued in their book *SuperFreakonomics: Global Cooling, Patriotic Prostitutes, and Why Suicide Bombers Should Buy Life Insurance*. The authors compare CO_2 to New York City's horse manure problem in the late nineteenth century. The number of horses had tripled from 1800 to 1870 and the streets were overflowing with excrement. The problem seemed insurmountable and the government proved incapable of regulating it. Just as things were becoming dire ... poof! Almost overnight horse manure became a non-issue as Americans began using automobiles.[234]

Less optimistic is Jason Hickel, an anthropologist at the London School of Economics and the author of *Less Is More: How Degrowth Will Save the World*, who has emerged as one of the leading spokespeople for what is known as the degrowth movement. To Hickel, the case for degrowth goes like this: The world is overproducing greenhouse gasses, overfishing, and overconsuming in dozens of unsustainable ways, from deforestation to plastic accumulating in the oceans. He argues that scientists have made impressive progress on technologies that should have been sufficient to address the climate crisis—think solar panels, meat alternatives, and eco-friendly houses. But because wealthy societies are so focused on growing the economy, those gains have been immediately plowed back into the economy, producing more stuff for the same ecological footprint but not shrinking the ecological footprint.[235]

Who should we listen to?

I find that the optimists have an almost evangelical faith in technology as our savior—which is ironic since both Pinker and Rosling compare environmentalists to religious fanatics. Given that climate change is already delivering fatal consequences, perhaps we shouldn't assume Elon Musk will deliver a *deus ex machina* just in the nick of time to save us. In addition, I have no desire to live on Mars. Instead, I feel we should put all our resources and energy into saving

Earth. Maybe the best thing coming out of space and Mars exploration is that we will finally realize how precious and fragile our blue marble is and that humanity is just hanging on by a tiny thread. Star Trek's Captain Kirk actor William Shatner described his "overwhelming sadness" and one of the strongest feelings of grief he has ever felt when coming back to Earth after a space visit with the Blue Origin space shuttle, stating, "When I landed back on Earth, I wept for the Earth because I realized it's dying."[236] I thought of this quote during a recent dive trip to Roatan, Honduras. For this first time, I witnessed with my own eyes the bleaching and dying of our coral reefs. The fact that the water temperature was 2 degrees celsius warmer than it should have been was poor consolation for the destruction of this beautiful, vital marine ecosystem. The world's oceans are our greatest carbon sink and will be the most ravaged by the warming of the planet. In the last 50 years we have lost more than 80 percent of our fish population due to dying reefs, overfishing, and runoffs from agricultural chemicals.[237]

Many optimistic assessments relate to the "environmental Kuznets curve," which shows that as countries get richer, they become cleaner. For example, if you compare Afghanistan and Bangladesh with Nordic countries, it is clear that indicators like air and water quality are much better in the latter. When you include carbon emissions and resource consumption, the ecological footprints of Afghanistan and Bangladesh—namely, the area required to provide the resources they use—are, respectively, 0.9 and 0.7 hectares per person. Norway's is 5.8, Sweden's is 6.5, and Finland's 6.7.[238] (Here I want to make it clear that I am not advocating we all adopt living standards comparable to those in Afghanistan and Bangladesh. As we will see, a certain level of material wealth is necessary for one's well-being, and countries the UN categorizes as "least developed," like Afghanistan, Haiti, and Cameroon, desperately need GDP growth.) Optimists also claim that we are already on the path to managing climate change through technological advancement, citing the leveling-off of domestic greenhouse gas emissions in wealthy countries in recent decades. In reality, trade statistics show that these countries simply exported their emissions along with their manufacturing to countries like China, where emissions ballooned.

So, in case it isn't clear by now, I think the dismissal of environmental concerns by champions of continued growth is a grave mistake. I also think their insistence that GDP growth fixes all problems is a mix of wishful thinking and often asserting causation where there's no evidence for it. All this being said, common sense tells us that going from $500 a year to $15,000 would drastically improve your quality of life. There is also robust evidence that it lowers population growth by increasing the cost of having children in terms of opportunity costs. It is the consumption in affluent countries like those in Western Europe and North America that has increased the global material footprint since the Industrial Revolution, and this is where we need to question the wisdom of an unending pursuit of economic growth. According to the Human Development Report, "Material footprint per capita in high-income countries is 60 percent higher than in upper-middle-income countries and more than 13 times the level of low-income countries."[239]

The important takeaway isn't that GDP is inherently bad, or that we should prevent low-income countries from growing economically. Rather, it is that GDP is being misused as an indicator of something it doesn't measure and was never intended to measure—the well-being of a nation. As I write this, the Biden administration is being attacked for altering the definition of "recession." Given our obsession with GDP growth, it's easy to understand why. In the Western world, we assume an unending correlation between happiness and income, but as we will see, there is more to life.

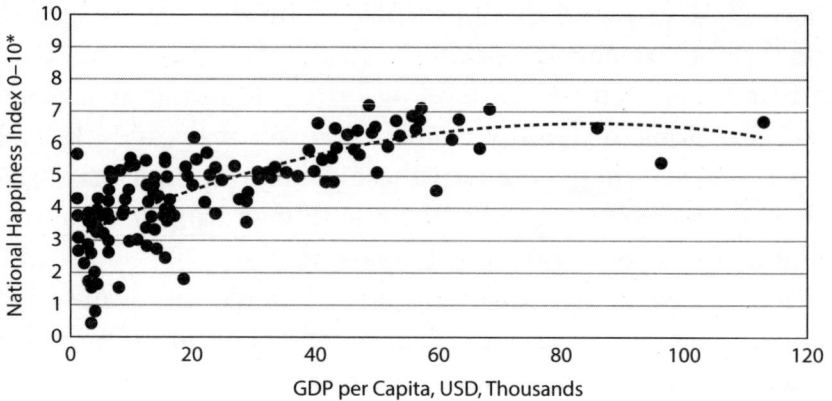

Figure 6.2 At a certain point, increased income no longer makes people happy
(*Source*: Shorders)[240]

Every year, the United Nations Sustainable Development Solutions Network releases the "World Happiness Report" assessing how happy the citizens of each nation are based on respondents rating their own lives. Its findings regularly reveal two important points that we should keep in mind.

The first is that although a basic level of material wealth is necessary, the relationship between wealth and happiness has its limits. As Figure 6.2 shows, happiness plateaus as the average income in a developed country reaches $70,000 per household.

The second is that a high GDP is not a prerequisite for happiness, nor does it guarantee it. Costa Rica is an excellent example of this.

The Costa Rican Approach

In 2020, Costa Rica had a per capita GDP of around $12,200, which was about 10 percent higher than the rest of the world. Comparatively, South Korea had a GDP of $31,600, which was about 65.5 percent higher than the rest of the world and

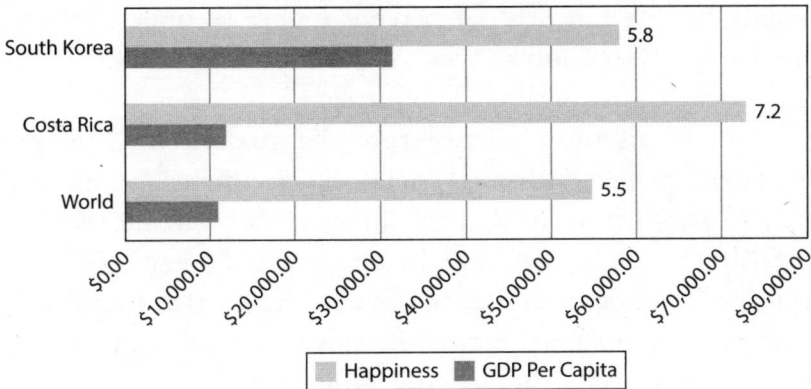

Figure 6.3 GDP doesn't necessarily increase happiness

61 percent higher than Costa Rica's.[241] Yet with a score of 7.2 (out of 10) on the happiness index, Costa Rica was the 12th happiest country while South Korea was the 57th with a score of 5.8 (see Figure 6.3). Despite being 61 percent poorer, Costa Ricans were 19 percent happier than Koreans. Overall, there were about 40 countries richer yet less happy than Costa Rica, including the USA, the UK, Italy, and Japan.[242]

Costa Rica's success is also reflected in the Social Progress Index (SPI), which its government has officially adopted to track progress on the national and municipal levels. Conceptualized by Harvard Business School Professor Michael Porter, the SPI measures the extent to which countries' public institutions are providing for their citizens. The SPI seeks to move beyond gross GDP as a given measure of progress, providing "a holistic, objective, transparent, outcome-based measure of a country's well-being that is independent of economic indicators." It is based on 52 indicators grouped into three broad conceptual dimensions defining social progress: Basic Human Needs, Foundations of Well-being, and Opportunity. With a score of 77.8, Costa Rica outperformed around 30 countries with higher GDPs. Saudi Arabia, for example, was ranked 41 spots lower despite having a nearly 74 percent higher income. (As usual, the five Nordic countries were at the top; the USA was ranked 24th—the lowest of the G7 countries.)

Costa Rica's success can largely be attributed to the government's prioritization of social development and environmental protection. It was the first country in the world to abolish its military and has since redirected defense spending to improve education and healthcare while also establishing a strong social safety net. Although Costa Rica's per-capita income is a sixth that of the United States—and its per-capita healthcare costs are a fraction of ours—life expectancy there is approaching 81 years. In the United States, life expectancy peaked in 2014 at just under 79 years and has declined since.[243] Meanwhile, the USA continues to spend more on defense than the next nine countries combined.

Costa Rica has also been a world leader in environmental protection. Its pioneering Payments for Environmental Services (PES) program pays landowners for the environmental services that their lands produce when adopting sustainable land-use and forest-management techniques. As a result, it is the only tropical country in the world that has reversed deforestation. The country generates more than 95 percent of its domestic electricity from renewable energy and is committed to achieving 100 percent electricity from renewable energy by 2030 and fully decarbonizing by 2050.[244]

As Michael Green, Executive Director of the US-based nonprofit organization Social Progress Imperative puts it, "The Social Progress Index proves that GDP is not destiny. We need more countries to be like Costa Rica, which squeezes a lot of social progress out of its modest GDP. Costa Rica has so much to teach the world."[245]

Finally, Costa Rica is the first country in the world to implement the Inner Development Goals (IDGs) framework to support and accelerate the UN's 17 SDGs. The IDGs were developed by Tomas Björkman and his team at the Swedish non-profit Ekskäret to develop people's inner capacity to better handle the world's increased complexity. According to Ekskäret:

> In 2015, the SDGs gave us a comprehensive plan for a sustainable world by 2030. The 17 goals cover a wide range of issues that involve people with different needs, values, and convictions. There is a vision of what needs to happen, but progress along this vision has so far been disappointing. We lack the inner capacity to deal with our increasingly complex environment and challenges. Fortunately, modern research shows that the inner abilities we now all need can be developed and values can be taught. This was the starting point for the 'Inner Development Goals' initiative.[246]

The idea originated from Tomas Björkman and Lene Andersen and their book *The Nordic Secret: A European Story of Beauty and Freedom*.[247]

When countries are ranked by the well-being of their citizens, most people expect to find Nordic countries at the top of the list, regardless of the metric being used to measure success, from healthcare to happiness. But few can explain why. This phenomenon is known as the "Nordic Secret."

As recently as the turn of the twentieth century, the Nordic countries were impoverished agricultural societies under authoritarian leadership. Today, Sweden, Norway, Denmark, Iceland, and Finland enjoy the highest standard of living, gender equality, and social justice in the world. As observed in the popular movie *Barbie* and the eye-opening book *Invisible Women* by Caroline Criado Perez, Sweden is close to a female utopia.[248]

If you asked a Swedish citizen why they care about gender equality, their answer would likely focus on more than just gender equality and women's family planning and reproductive rights. That's a given. Instead, they might attribute it to not identifying solely as Swedish but rather as global citizens interested in human rights, who happen to be Swedish.

As we're seeing across the globe today, in times of uncertainty and rapid change, people tend to lean toward authoritarian leaders to anchor themselves, with devastating consequences of isolationism and tribal mentalities instead of international collaboration and cooperation. The need to anchor ourselves based on our inner compass and become "self-authoring" has never been more important. The Nordic countries did exactly that, and it is reflected in all the Nordic countries today. This is their secret.

Take Sweden, for example. In 1857, at a time of rapid change and uncertainty, the country transformed its population through educational initiatives focused on inner secular consciousness. This in turn stabilized democracy and avoided civil unrest, allowing rapid change to occur peacefully. Sweden educated its citizens to think for themselves and allow their own values and purposes to guide them, thus becoming grounded and the authors of their own lives. This education was called "Bildung." "Bildung" offered a combination of education and knowledge necessary to gain moral and emotional maturity as a group member with strong individual autonomy—a skill necessary to thrive in society and directly linked to the success of the Nordic countries.

The result of "Bildung" quickly became apparent. People began caring about those outside their typical circles, and quickly their circles started expanding to include those with different religious beliefs, demographics, and cultural backgrounds. This opened people up to the fact that we live in a complex and interconnected world. This was a key component in fostering a sense of belonging and the curiosity needed to open up minds to the diverse world we live in. I fondly remember learning about all the world religions in school growing up in Sweden, fostering in me an inclusive and worldly view of our diverse human belief systems.

Looking at Figure 6.4, our perspective and connection need to evolve to where all the circles are included. We need to open up our mind and focus on larger circles than the "self." It is in the outer circle of inclusion, "the extended family" as the indigenous people call it, that you will find meaning and more hope for the future and peace. All our tribal, religious, racial, national, and ideological divisions have been constructed by men in power. The "us vs. them" mentality fosters fear, allowing the "alpha" males to maintain their positions as perceived protectors. These leaders operate on a level focused only on self interest, with a very limited worldview and with a lack of

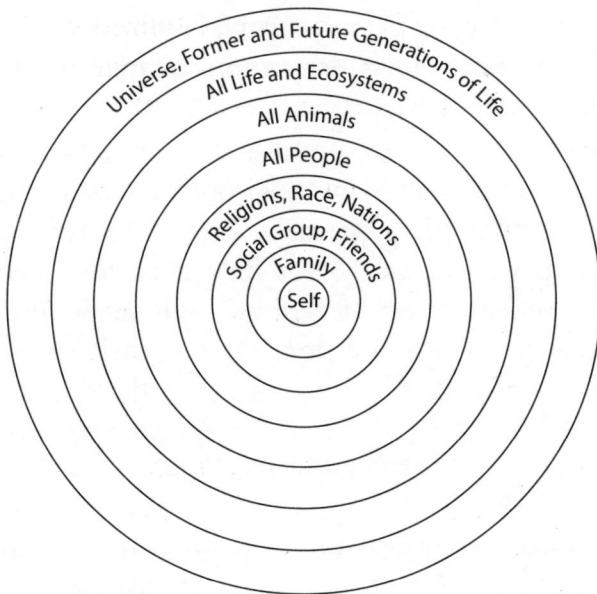

Figure 6.4 Circles of connection

connection to anything larger than themselves. The polycrisis is the consequence to this limited type of leadership mindset.

Today, newborns around the world, including in the USA, are born with "forever" chemicals in their systems. In 2005, the American Red Cross collected 10 samples of newborn umbilical cord blood and found an average of 287 chemicals present—180 of which cause cancer, 217 are toxic to the brain and nervous system, and 208 can cause birth defects.[249] By 2022, "forever" chemicals were detected in all 300,000 newborn samples of umbilical cord blood analyzed in 40 studies.

The question arises: Should our worry be directed toward "them" or should we focus on what is actually harming us?

For a hopeful future, it's imperative that we fortify our inner foundation and balance of the masculine and feminine. Doing so could reduce the allure of authoritarian masculine figures who claim to have all the answers, whether he is a national leader, a CEO, or a religious guru. These leaders aim to narrow our perspectives, making us more manageable. They tap into our primal survival instincts by convincing their followers that they alone can protect society from "enemies" intent on its destruction.

We all possess an inner moral guide, compass, and anchor. The real question is, when will we start utilizing them?

Herein lie humanity's greatest strengths: our diversity of thought, experiences, and knowledge; our untapped potential; and, ironically, our "freedom"—all of which are more important now than ever before.

The Bhutan Approach

Costa Rica isn't the only country that has moved away from a GDP-centric definition of progress. Situated deep in the eastern Himalayan mountains, Bhutan is often overshadowed by its more prominent neighbors, China and India. Despite its small size, the country regularly makes headlines for a variety of socioeconomic achievements. Bhutan remains, for example, the first and only carbon-negative country in the world. It also managed to prevent the Covid-19 pandemic from overwhelming its population, with only one Bhutanese citizen passing away from the virus at the time of writing.

What truly sets Bhutan apart, however, is its switch from a GDP-based measure of progress to one focused on Gross National Happiness (GNH). The phrase was first coined by the fourth King of Bhutan, King Jigme Singye Wangchuck, in 1972 when he declared, "Gross National Happiness is more important than Gross Domestic Product"—a both wise and obvious sentiment, yet one that would be political suicide in the Western world.

The basic idea behind GNH is that the government should take a holistic approach toward notions of progress and give equal importance to non-economic aspects of well-being. It assesses happiness based on four pillars broken into nine domains evaluated by 33 indicators. The four pillars and nine domains are:

1. Sustainable and equitable socioeconomic development.
   - Living standards: Measuring Bhutanese citizens' basic economic condition.
   - Health: Measuring the country's physical health status.
   - Education: Measuring several factors, including participation, skills, and educational support.

2. Preservation and promotion of a free and resilient culture.
   - Cultural diversity and resilience: Measuring the diversity and strength of cultural traditions in Bhutan.

- Community vitality: Measuring the strengths and weaknesses of relationships and interaction within communities.
- Time use: Analyzing how citizens spend their time.
- Psychological well-being: Encompassing contentment or satisfaction with various aspects of life and health of the mind.

3. Ecological sustainability.

- Ecological diversity and resilience: Assesses the state of natural resources, the pressures on ecosystems, and different management responses.

4. Good governance and equality before the law.

- Good governance: Evaluates participation in decision-making, effectiveness of government, just and equal law, freedom and quality of media, and transparency, accountability, honesty, or corruption.[250]

Since 2008, all legislation that passes through the Bhutanese government must be filtered through a "GNH policy lens," meaning every policy decision has operated under the pretense of raising GNH rather than GDP. Since the GNH became a guiding force of public policy, the country has made remarkable gains.[251] According to a World Bank report, poverty rates fell from 36 percent to 12 percent between 2007 and 2017, the steepest decline witnessed in Southeast Asia.[252] During this same period, enrollment in primary education skyrocketed by 30 percent, with significant gains in secondary education as well. In terms of infrastructure, 91 percent of the Bhutanese population now lives within a one-hour distance of a health facility compared with just 73 percent in 2007, while greater public investment increased farm road networks from 1,700 km to 11,200 km between 2008 and 2017.[253]

Like Costa Rica, Bhutan has recognized the relationship between well-being and the natural world and has enshrined environmental protection into the constitution. The country has pledged to remain carbon neutral and to ensure that at least 60 percent of its landmass will remain under forest cover in perpetuity. It has banned export logging and has even instigated a monthly pedestrian day that bans all private vehicles from its roads. As Thakur Singh Powdyel, Bhutan's former minister of education, observed, "It's easy to mine the land and fish the seas and get rich. Yet we believe you cannot have a prosperous nation in the long run that does not conserve its natural environment or take care of the well-being of its people, which is being borne out by what is happening to the outside world."[254]

The Sustainable Development Goals as Our "North Star"

It is a promising sign to see more and more countries using the UN's Sustainable Development Goals as a "North Star" guiding policy decisions. My hope is that businesses will follow suit. This is a trend that provides a glimmer of hope for a brighter future. It is worth diving a bit more into the SDGs and why we should do everything we can to accelerate this trend.

At the heart, the SDGs are a global commitment to addressing some of the most pressing challenges facing humanity. Adopted by all United Nations Member States in 2015, the 17 goals encompass a broad range of interconnected issues, including poverty, hunger, health, education, gender equality, clean water, sanitation, and climate action. The importance of the SDGs lies in their comprehensive and integrated approach to sustainable development, aiming to create a more equitable, resilient, and environmentally sustainable world.

One key significance of the SDGs is their universality. Unlike their predecessor, the Millennium Development Goals (MDGs), the SDGs apply to all countries, regardless of their level of development. This acknowledges the interconnectedness of global challenges and emphasizes the shared responsibility of all nations to work toward a common agenda. By fostering international collaboration and cooperation, the SDGs provide a framework for addressing transboundary issues such as climate change, biodiversity loss, and infectious diseases that require collective action on a global scale.

Importantly, the SDGs prioritize inclusivity, leaving no one behind. The goals explicitly recognize the importance of addressing disparities and ensuring that the benefits of development reach all segments of society, including the most vulnerable and marginalized. This commitment to inclusivity reflects a departure from traditional development approaches that may have inadvertently perpetuated inequality. By focusing on social equity and justice, the SDGs aim to build societies in which everyone has the opportunity to thrive, regardless of their background or circumstances.

Economic sustainability—rather than a singular focus on GDP growth—is another crucial aspect of the SDGs. The goals recognize the need for economic development that is environmentally responsible and socially inclusive. This involves promoting sustainable consumption and production patterns, fostering innovation, and ensuring that economic growth does not come at the expense of environmental degradation. By integrating economic, social, and environmental dimensions, the SDGs strive to create a holistic and balanced approach to development that promotes long-term well-being.

Education plays a central role in the SDGs and is seen as a key driver of progress across all dimensions of sustainable development. Goal 4 focuses explicitly on ensuring inclusive and equitable quality education for all. Education not only empowers individuals and communities but also serves as a catalyst for achieving other goals, such as poverty eradication, improved health, and gender equality. Education is also the strongest link to stabilize democracy. Through education, societies can develop the knowledge and skills needed to address complex challenges and foster a culture of sustainability.

Climate action, encapsulated in Goal 13, is another crucial aspect of the SDGs. The urgent need to mitigate climate change and adapt to its impacts is woven throughout the goals, recognizing the profound influence of environmental factors on social and economic well-being. By setting ambitious targets for reducing greenhouse gas emissions, increasing resilience, and mobilizing financial resources for climate-related projects, the SDGs aim to contribute to a sustainable and climate-resilient future.

Overall, the importance of the SDGs lies in their ability to provide a comprehensive, universal, and integrated framework for addressing the multifaceted challenges facing the world. By promoting collaboration, inclusivity, economic sustainability, education, and climate action, the SDGs offer a roadmap for building a more equitable, resilient, and sustainable world for current and future generations. Achieving these goals requires collective effort, political will, and a commitment to leaving no one behind, emphasizing the shared responsibility of the global community in shaping a better future for all. Whether you are a government official, CEO, or community organizer, all leaders should familiarize themselves with the SDG framework. If humanity fails the SDGs, it fails itself and the future begins to look incredibly bleak. Unfortunately, like the goals for the Paris Climate accords, at our current trajectory we are unlikely to reach the 2030 SDG targets. It is not too late to change this, but each day brings us closer to the point of no return.

As touched on, Costa Rica has embraced the IDG framework. This is a trend that should be embraced among leaders everywhere. Sadly, most don't have the consciousness or caring to adequately address the world's most pressing problems. This is a sign that the majority become leaders for the wrong reasons, valuing power above all else and turning care for others into an afterthought. This needs to change and will require collective action to do so. As highlighted in Chapter 3, toxic leaders such as Putin, Trump, and Le Pen are more dangerous now than ever before. The reason why the IDGs are so important is that they develop our inner abilities and values to combat "the laissez-faire" attitude that allows bad leaders to remain in power. They offer the potential to bring about the leadership evolution we so desperately need by increasing our understanding of the world's complexity and our inner capacity to deal with it.

Conclusion

In the last several decades, economic growth in countries such as China and India has unequivocally improved the quality of life for billions of people, allowing them to live longer and healthier lives. The sustainability of it remains to be seen. What is clear, however, is that a high GDP is not a prerequisite for well-being or a remedy for low-income countries, nor will it buy happiness in wealthier ones. Too often, world leaders have used it as a get-out-of-jail-free card that excuses environmental destruction or authoritarianism. As Costa Rica and Bhutan teach us, there is more to life and leadership than economic growth. By looking beyond income, both countries have drastically improved the happiness and well-being of their citizens while protecting their environment and strengthening democratic institutions.

Though more countries are beginning to follow their lead, our national leaders still prioritize accelerating GDP growth above other concerns, just like corporate leaders prioritize quarterly profits. And when this happens, they lose sight of what truly matters—long, healthy, meaningful lives.

They follow the religion of GDP, increasing the chances for disastrous consequences. This happens because GDP rewards production and consumption, not societal or environmental well-being. If we aren't careful, our singular obsession with GDP growth will lead us to an environmentally bleak future with increasing rates of human suffering and inequality. The obsession will push us to destroy everything that is priceless and irreplaceable.

As we progress through the most pivotal decade in human history, it is clear that we can no longer rely on GDP alone to measure the quality and effectiveness of our leaders; we can no longer be seduced by the promise of higher incomes. As Robert F. Kennedy said in a speech at the University of Kansas in 1968:

> Our Gross National Product … counts air pollution, cigarette advertising, and ambulances to clear our highways of carnage. … It counts the destruction of the redwood and the loss of our natural wonder … [T]he Gross National Product does not allow for the health of our children, the quality of their education, or the joy of their play. It does not include the beauty of our poetry … the intelligence of our public debate, or the integrity of our public officials. It measures neither our wit nor our courage, neither our wisdom nor our learning … it measures everything, in short, except that which makes life worthwhile.[255]

Ask Yourself

How will your next purchase and consumption lead to well-being in your life?

Don't Underestimate the Human Potential

One of my motivations to write this book stemmed from my belief that we are living in a defining moment in human history. As mentioned, if humanity's story were a 1,000-page book, the vast majority of it would be, for lack of a better word, boring. Recorded history doesn't even start until around page 775. Things progress slowly from there. Irrigation comes along, then gunpowder, and the printing press. The reader would think to themselves, "Finally, something is happening," but it is still far from a page-turner. On the last page, however, the book turns haywire. Humans travel into space and build the Large Hadron Collider. The atmosphere starts to warm and biodiversity declines. From pages one to 999, the human population was under one billion. On page 1,000, it is eight billion. Something is happening.[256]

To avoid the catastrophes highlighted in Chapter 1, we need a new way of thinking and governance. Given our god-like powers going into page 1,001, we need it before things go wrong. Human history generally follows a pattern: good times create foolish people, which leads to bad times, creating wise people, and the cycle starts over again.

The last few decades have, in many ways, been "the best of times." Since World War II—arguably the worst thing that has ever happened to our species—humanity has been enjoying what is known as the "long peace." Until quite recently, as long as there have been Germans and French, they have had few qualms about killing each other. Today, war between the two nations isn't even discussed, not because it isn't in the strategic interests of either country but because it is absurd. If both heads of state gave impassioned speeches declaring war on each other, their citizens would likely respond not with a burst of patriotic militarism but with amused bewilderment. The two leaders would not only be ignored but promptly checked for any mental deficiency. Overall, more people than ever before are privileged to live their lives in unprecedented comfort.

The question now is, how do we steer clear of the storm clouds on the horizon? We know the consequences of pumping carbon into the atmosphere, yet we continue to do so as the world burns before our very eyes. We allow corporations to steamroll ahead with little to no oversight, developing technologies with the potential to cause our extinction, while in the process destroying our planet. And we elect leaders who tap into our primitive emotions and propagate blatant lies, such as immigrants are the problem, well-established science is a hoax, or more guns lead to less gun violence.

A 2021 poll by the Public Religion Research Institute and the Interfaith Youth Core found that 15 percent of Americans say they think that the levers of power are controlled by a cabal of Satan-worshiping pedophiles. The same share said it was true that "American patriots may have to resort to violence" to depose the pedophiles and restore the country's rightful order.[257]

I think Toby Ord captures our current predicament quite nicely in his observation that. "As the gap between our power and our wisdom grows, our future is subject to an ever-increasing level of risk. This situation is unsustainable."

Optimists often highlight that rationality has rarely been a hallmark of human behavior. Yuval Harari has pointed out that for millennia, the bulk of what was considered "news" and "facts" in human societies comprised tales of miracles, angels, demons, and witches, with audacious narrators providing live coverage from the underworld's depths.[258] Our world is fundamentally shaped by stories, with some enduring for thousands of years to maintain a strong sense of belonging within human groups. These narratives drive our values and cultures. However, the stories asserting the superiority of one gender, the existence of only two genders (Adam and Eve), or the notion that a particular ethnic group or nation is "chosen" by a divine being are antiquated and no longer beneficial. When a story perpetuates intolerance and hatred toward another gender, ethnic group, or nation, it's time for that story to be abandoned. "Morality" doesn't mean "following divine commands." It means "reducing suffering."[259] Hence, in order to act morally, you don't need to believe in any myth or story, you just need to develop a deep appreciation for suffering. To build a livable, meaningful future, we must start telling ourselves better stories. Stories were women are in power and more importantly feminine wisdom is valued and celebrated. It's essential to recognize that for those in power, ancient narratives are incredibly effective tools for keeping the "in-group" fearful of the "out-group," thus ensuring compliance and maintaining their power.

Two narratives from Judeo-Christian biblical teachings underscore this: the acceptance of slavery (Leviticus 25:44–46) and the concept of fathers selling their daughters into slavery (Exodus 21:7) serve as stark reminders of the deeply entrenched patriarchal narratives of the past. Perhaps the most appalling story, which involves the killing of innocent newborns (Exodus 11:4–5), prompts us to question the values it promotes. Does this narrative embody inclusiveness, compassion, and love, or does it evoke hate, killing, and war? This invites reflection on the nature of divinity. Interestingly, these narratives are relatively recent, dating back only 2,000–3,000 years. Visiting Olduvai Gorge in East Africa, the cradle of human evolution,

I was struck by the thought of the stories humans must have told themselves over more than 198,000 years, long before the advent of these holy stories.

Regardless, we should be improving in this regard, not backsliding. If you went back to 1995 and tried to explain to Americans that in 30 years there would be a flourishing flat earth movement and a political cult based on the idea that Donald Trump is fighting a cabal of pedophile Satanists, people would likely think you were the one who had lost your mind.

Ukraine is one country that doesn't need to be reminded that there is still plenty of foolishness in the world, which is in the unfortunate position of having a very powerful and very foolish neighbor. Former world chess champion Garry Kasparov and other Russian dissidents suggest Russian President Vladimir Putin's aggression against Ukraine is explainable only as an attempt to fulfill an imperialist fantasy.

According to Kasparov, in speeches to the Russian Duma, Putin tends to invoke "a screed of ahistorical grievances" to claim that Ukraine is rightfully Russia's.[260] In a speech in June 2022, Putin made this difficult to deny after comparing himself to the eighteenth-century Russian tsar Peter the Great, drawing a parallel between what he portrayed as their twin historic quests to win back Russian land.

Needless to say, taking a nation to war to insinuate an eighteenth-century tsar is a very foolish thing to do. Of course, there have always been madmen in the world happy to sacrifice blood and treasure for their delusions of grandeur. However, leaders like Putin didn't become leaders overnight. Putin rose to power in an environment and leadership culture that allowed him to. The war in Ukraine shows us that there still are and that we haven't quite entered an era of pristine wisdom. This should worry us all because as our intelligence grows, so does our power. And if our leaders are still capable of acting so foolishly, the consequences are increasingly less likely to be isolated and temporary.

Wisdom refers to the qualities of having experience, knowledge, and good judgment. This differs from "intelligence," which is the ability to acquire and apply knowledge and skills. Intelligence is what allowed us to build nuclear weapons. Wisdom is what prevented us from using them (so far) since Nagasaki and Hiroshima.

In a patriarchal-dominated world, caring for people outside of their in-group as well as the environment is not a priority. In contrast, people and the environment are leveraged to benefit the men on top.

"Drill, baby, drill!" We've all heard it before. It's one of Donald Trump's favorite slogans. This is no coincidence. The fossil fuel industry invests hundreds of millions each year in lobbying efforts. Trump's 2024 Presidential Campaign was funded by $445 million dollars from the fossil fuel industry.[261] However, the industry faces a potentially existential threat due to the free market. Renewable energy is clean, reliable, and, as of 2020, the cheapest form of energy available.[262]

Meanwhile, the fossil fuel industry is increasingly reliant on government handouts, with US taxpayers paying $20 billion per year to make fossil fuels "affordable." Globally, this figure reaches $1 trillion.[263] The real cost, however, is the harm it does to our water, soil, and air, and its' devastating effects on our health and the well-being of all forms of life.

Trump has appointed Lee Zeldin to lead the Environmental Protection Agency (EPA), a federal agency responsible for protecting the environment and human health. It is well known that Zeldin has deep ties to Texas fracking billionaire Tim Dunn.[264] How is conflict of interest prevented?

As the Southern California wildfires at the beginning of 2025 once again demonstrated, we are also paying a price in the form of wildfires, floods, and droughts. As mentioned at the start of this book, one would think that the 8.7 million premature deaths each year directly linked to oil and gas would be enough to pause drilling.[265] But it is not. I ask you, the reader, is it right to continue to deregulate and subsidize the fossil fuel industry in light of what is taking place? Where you land on the political spectrum should be irrelevant. Moreover, renewable energy is projected to become a $23 trillion industry by 2030, accelerating the creation of millions of well-paying, stable jobs and supporting opportunities in communities across the country.[266] It already employs three times more workers than those associated with traditional energy, and this number is growing.[267] I believe we can all agree—left, right, and everything in between—that renewable energy is simply a necessity if the USA is to stay relevant in the global economy.

We are in dire need of wiser leaders—leaders who embody compassion, care, and nurturing qualities, and who excel in collaboration, cooperation, and coordination. This need spans across all sectors, both private and public. I firmly believe that embracing better leadership is crucial for our future, and it's time to fully leverage the skills, perspectives, and wisdom of our entire human race. In this endeavor, women play a pivotal role in safely steering us through the looming challenges.

Research supports the notion that increasing women's representation in politics leads to more effective governance while diminishing corruption. The Nordic countries serve as a prime example, boasting the highest rates of female leadership globally, with political representation nearing 50 percent. It's no coincidence that these nations also lead the world in environmental initiatives. Indeed, the status of women in a society, rather than its GDP, is a more accurate predictor of the country's quality of life. Women, by their nature, tend to be less violent and more nurturing. It's noteworthy that humans exhibit aggression six times more than the average mammal, with men accounting for 90–96 percent of global homicides. The last century witnessed the deaths of 85 million men, women, and children in mass killings and genocides, a cycle of violence we say "never again" to, only to see it recur.[268, 269, 270] The root cause? The toxic male patriarchy.

Rwanda's story post-1994 genocide is a testament to the power of female leadership. I visited the genocide museum in Kigali in 2009, only 15 years after more than one million people were slaughtered in 100 days, yet Rwanda has emerged as a beacon of survival, resilience, and peace. Women were at the forefront of rebuilding the nation—taking in orphans, supporting widows, transitioning from cleaners to constructors, and starting businesses. Their efforts brought stability in the wake of horrific violence. Aloisea Inyumba, a notable female leader, played a crucial role in rehoming orphans and promoting adoption without ethnic bias. In 2003, Rwanda enshrined gender equality in its constitution, ensuring at least 30 percent female representation in leadership. Today, with women constituting 64 percent of its elected officials—the highest globally—Rwanda stands as a twenty-first-century success story, showcasing stability, low corruption, and significant progress.[271]

Aggression in leadership must cease to be tolerated or celebrated. Let's call for an end to this era dominated by aggressive, bully-like leaders. It falls upon each of us, as followers, to reject and call out such leadership styles. As a leadership consultant and coach, I witness and confront these behaviors daily in the workplace.

Incorporating women into leadership roles not only reduces the likelihood of violent conflicts but also increases the chances of peaceful resolutions to ongoing disputes. Studies have shown that nations with higher levels of gender equality are more inclined to resolve conflicts non-violently and are less likely to engage in military actions to settle international disagreements. Conversely, countries with significant gender disparities often experience more internal and external conflicts. This evidence underscores the critical need for gender-balanced leadership in fostering a more peaceful and equitable world.[272]

As Albert Einstein once said, "We cannot solve our problems with the same thinking we used to create them."[273]

It is not about promoting women at the expense of men, but rather about embracing a more balanced approach to leadership. We need to recognize that both masculine and feminine qualities are necessary for effective leadership and that a combination of the two can create a more holistic and sustainable approach to governance. This is not just about gender, but about changing the way we think about leadership and power. To quote educator and leadership philosopher Sudhanshu Palsule, "Humanity has created a monolithic idea of leadership that has made the rest of us silent."[274]

Ultimately, the defining moment in human history that we are living in requires us to think differently and act differently. It requires us to recognize the interconnectedness of our world and the importance of empathy, compassion, and collaboration in addressing the challenges we face. By embracing a more balanced approach to leadership and empowering women to play a greater role in shaping our collective future, we can create a more just, equitable, and sustainable world for all. We will not reach our human potential with half of humanity, women, currently at the sidelines. As mentioned, at the current rate with gender equality vanishing before our eyes, it will take another 300 years to reach gender equality—we simply don't have 300 years to get this right.

It is entirely possible to build an ideal society, free of violence, destitution, and extreme inequality, with humans living in harmony with each other and with the natural world. To achieve this, a prerequisite is recognizing that we are all in it together and that we need to start caring for one another, whether you are a woman or man, Democrat or Republican, rich or poor, white or Black, American or Russian, Christian or Muslim. It is about *being a good human above all*, and it is our unique diversity and collaboration that are going to realize the greatest potential in humanity. Diversity is the key ingredient to resilience and has ensured the survival of natural ecosystems for millions of years.[275] How much better this world could be is something, in my opinion, most people underestimate. We can simply no longer allow for masculine to dominate feminine. Masculinity unchecked is dysfunctional and it is destroying us and everything worth living for.

In conclusion, I want to turn to a slightly altered version of the old parable *The Tale of Two Wolves*. The story is about a child who, one night, notices his grandpa sitting quietly by the fire. Earlier that day, the old man was assaulted by a younger man in a nearby village. Surely, thinks the child, he must be plotting his revenge. After approaching him to ask what he has in store for the man, the grandpa blinks and asks his young grandson to sit down. Instead, he tells him about a terrible battle that is raging within him—the battle between two wolves. The Wolf of Power is characterized by competition, influence, status, titles, wealth, and dominance. The Wolf of Wisdom, by cooperation, love, compassion, kindness, generosity, hope, and a desire for peace. "The same horrible fight is going on within you, my child, and every person on Earth since the beginning of time," Grandpa says and falls silent. His grandson's eyes grow. "But which wolf will survive?" he asks. "The one you feed," Grandpa replies.

Looking at the world today, it's clear that since the Industrial Revolution the Wolf of Power has become obese while the Wolf of Wisdom malnourished. If we are to advance humanity and ensure our planet's survival, we need to reconcile the battle within us and lead the world to a better place.

The narrative that "Humans have always been this way and always will be," or that "Violence is human nature, there will always be wars" paints a bleak picture of our species, one mired in endless cycles of violence. Yet, this perspective overlooks our equally innate capacity for profound love and compassion. The prevalence of violence and conflict throughout history can, in part, be attributed to the millennia of unchecked dominance by patriarchal values and authoritarian leaders representing a small subset of humanity. Leading to a skewed representation of what it means to be human. Toby Ord, in his poignant observation, highlights the precariousness of our current trajectory: "As the gap between our power and wisdom widens, our future faces an ever-increasing level of risk. The situation is unsustainable."[276] This statement serves as an urgent call to redefine our collective path: we need a new story.

The notion that our story must end in tragedy, defined by our worst impulses, is a narrative we must reject. We are beings of remarkable potential, capable of reshaping our destiny through acts of courage, wisdom, and empathy. The era of leadership characterized by narrow-mindedness, self-interest, and authoritarianism must come to an end. As long as these outdated models prevail, the suffering of our people and the degradation of our planet will continue unabated.

It's time to usher in a new era of leadership—one that reflects the diversity, complexity, and compassion of humanity itself. This new paradigm will be marked by a full representation of humanity leading humanity, who prioritize the well-being of their communities and the health of our planet over personal or corporate gain and power. In such a world, the best of humanity can flourish, leading to advancements and achievements we can only imagine.

Our world may never be perfect, but how much better this world could be is, in my opinion, highly underestimated. The future can be brighter, more just, and more peaceful than we've allowed ourselves to believe, in an environment free of pollutants. The best of humanity is yet to come, and it is a future we can create and celebrate together. In doing so, we will be proud not only of what we have accomplished but also of who we have become.

Ask Yourself

Which wolf do you feed?

End Notes

1 Usha C. V. Haley and George T. Haley, *Subsidies to Chinese Industry: State Capitalism, Business Strategy, and Trade Policy* (New York: Oxford University Press, 2013), v.

2 Charles Dickens, *A Tale of Two Cities* (London: Chapman & Hill, Wordsworth Editions, 1993), 1.

3 "Decline of global extreme poverty continues but has slowed: World Bank," World Bank Group, September 19, 2018, https://www.worldbank.org/en/news/press-release/2018/09/19/decline-of-global-extreme-poverty-continues-but-has-slowed-world-bank#:~:text=WASHINGTON%2C%20Sept.,investments%2C%20the%20World%20Bank%20finds.

4 Bastian Herre, Lucas Rodés-Guirao, Max Roser, Joe Hasell, and Bobbie Macdonald, "War and Peace," *Our World in Data*, August 7, 2024.

5 Steven Pinker, "Violence Vanquished," *The Wall Street Journal*, September 24, 2011.

6 Steven Pinker, *The Better Angels of Our Nature: Why Violence Has Declined* (London: Penguin, 2012).

7 Hans Rosling, *Factfulness: Ten Reasons We're Wrong About the World—And Why Things Are Better Than You Think* (London: Sceptre, 2018).

8 Charles Kenny, *Getting Better: Why Global Development Is Succeeding—And How We Can Improve the World Even More* (New York: Basic Books, 2011).

9 John Gramlich, "Looking Ahead to 2050, Americans Are Pessimistic About Many Aspects of Life in U.S.," Pew Research Center, March 21, 2019, https://www.pewresearch.org/short-reads/2019/03/21/looking-ahead-to-2050-americans-are-pessimistic-about-many-aspects-of-life-in-u-s/

10 Ray Kurzweil, "The Law of Accelerating Returns." In: Teuscher, C. (ed.), *Alan Turing: Life and Legacy of a Great Thinker* (Berlin, Heidelberg: Springer-Verlag, 2004), 381.

11 Tim Urban, *"The Artificial Intelligence Revolution: Part 1,"* Wait But Why (blog), January 22, 2015.

12 Toby Ord, *The Precipice: Existential Risk and the Future of Humanity* (New York: Hachette Book Group, 2020), 3–4.

13 Nico Grant and Karen Weise, "In A.I. Race, Microsoft and Google Choose Speed Over Caution," *The New York Times*, April 10, 2023.

14 Pat Swet, "Corporations Dominate World's Top 100 Economic Entities," *Business and Accountancy Daily*, September 14, 2016.

15 "Forests and the Biodiversity Convention: Independent Monitoring of the Implementation of the Expanded Programme of Work in Cameroon," Global Forest Coalition, May 2008, https://www.globalforestcoalition.org/wp-content/uploads/2010/11/IM-Report-Cameroon.pdf

16 "Cameroon Deforestation Rates & Statistics," GFW. Accessed August 16, 2024, https://www.globalforestwatch.org/dashboards/country/CMR/

17 Rodrigue Ngonzo, "Forest Voices: 'I don't have a problem with logging companies: I just want them to log according to the law," *Voices of the Forest*, January 18, 2021.

18 "Corporations Dominate World's Top 100 Economic Entities," *Business and Accountancy Daily*, September 14, 2016.

19 Richard Fuller, Philip J. Landrigan, Kalpana Balakrishnan, Glynda Bathan, Stephan Bose-O'Reilly, Michael Brauer et al., "Pollution and Health: A Progress Update," *The Lancet Planetary Health* 6, no. 6 (May 2022): 535–547.

20 "COVID – Coronavirus Statistics," Worldometer, last modified April 13, 2024, https://www.worldometers.info/coronavirus/

21 Linda Robinson and Noel James, "Women's Power Index," Council on Foreign Relations, last updated March 14, 2024, https://www.cfr.org/article/womens-power-index

22 Goal 5: Achieve Gender Equality and Empower All Women and Girls," United Nations, https://www.un.org/sustainabledevelopment/gender-equality/#:~:text=At%20the%20current%20rate%2C%20it,achieve%20equal%20representation%20in%20national

23 https://www.goodreads.com/quotes/9723699-the-last-thing-a-teacher-needs-to-give-her-pupils

24 Evan Osnos, "Doomsday Prep for the Super-Rich," *The New Yorker*, January 22, 2017, https://www.newyorker.com/magazine/2017/01/30/doomsday-prep-for-the-super-rich

25 Marjorie Garvey, Shelli Avenevoli, and Kathleen Anderson, "The National Institute of Mental Health Research Domain Criteria and Clinical Research in Child and Adolescent Psychiatry," *Journal of the American Academy of Child & Adolescent Psychiatry* 55, no. 2 (February 2016): 93–98.

26 Caroline Hickman, Elizabeth Marks, Panu Pihkala, Susan Clayton, R. Eric Lewandowski, Elouise E. Mayall, Britt Wray, Catriona Mellor, and Lise van Susteren, "Climate Anxiety in Children and Young People and Their Beliefs about Government Responses to Climate Change: A Global Survey," *The Lancet Planetary Health* 5, no. 12 (December 2021): 863–873.

27 Rutger Bregman, *Humankind: A Hopeful History* (UK: Bloomsbury Publishing, 2020), 6.

28 Steven Pinker, *The Better Angels of Our Nature: Why Violence Has Declined* (Penguin Books, 2012), xxii.

29 Laura Jacobs, Alyt Damstra, Mark Boukes, and Knut De Swert, "Back to Reality: The Complex Relationship Between Patterns in Immigration News Coverage and Real-World Developments in Dutch and Flemish Newspapers (1999–2015)," *Mass Communication and Society* 21, no. 4 (March 2018): 473–497.

30 https://www.brainyquote.com/quotes/john_c_maxwell_600859

31 Carl Sagan, "Nuclear War and Climatic Catastrophe: Some Policy Implications," *Foreign Affairs* 62, no. 2 (1983): 257–292.

32 Toby Ord, *The Precipice: Existential Risk and the Future of Humanity* (New York: Hachette Book Group, 2020), 45–46.

33 Toby Ord, *The Precipice: Existential Risk and the Future of Humanity* (New York: Hachette Book Group, 2020), 61.

34 Climate Central, based on IPCC AR6 WGI Chapter 3 (2021) Observed global surface temperature anomalies relative to 1850–1900 (white). Modeled effects of combined human and natural forcings (orange: including GHG emissions and aerosols); natural forcings only (green: solar activity and volcano emissions). Bands: 5–95% range of models.

35 Aatish Bhatia, "The Rate of Change: July 15, 2019," The Rate of Change (blog), July 15, 2019, https://rateofchange.substack.com/p/the-rate-of-change-july-15-2019

36 Center for Climate and Energy Solutions, "Changes in the Climate," https://www.c2es.org/content/changes-in-climate/#:~:text=The%20

Earth%20is%20Warming,but%20one%20happened%20since%20
2005

37 ResearchGate, "A tweet by National Review on December 14, 2015
showing the change in global temperature over time." [screenshot]
https://www.researchgate.net/figure/A-tweet-by-National-Review-
on-December-14-2015-showing-the-change-in-global-temperature_
fig1_321757804

38 National Oceanic and Atmospheric Administration, NOAA, "2024
was the world's warmest year on record" Jan 10, 2025, https://www.
noaa.gov/news/2024-was-worlds-warmest-year-on-record#
:~:text=Climate%20by%20the%20numbers,NOAA's%201850%
2D2024%20climate%20record.

39 "2023: Earth's Hottest Year on Record," *Climate Central*, January 12,
2024, https://www.climatecentral.org/climate-matters/2023-earths-
hottest-year-on-record

40 Minyvonne Burke and Liz Kreutz, "What We Know About the
Victims Killed in the California Wildfires," NBC NEWS, Feb 12,
2025.

41 Anna Betts and Tom Bryant, "LA Fires Live, January 13, 2025,"
https://www.theguardian.com/us-news/live/2025/jan/13/la-fire-wild-
fire-live-california-palisades-wind-santa-ana-gavin-newsom-latest-
usa-updates

42 Anthony Arguez, Shannan Hurley, Anand Inamdar, Laurel Mahoney,
Ahira Sanchez-Lugo, and Lilian Yang, "Should We Expect Each Year
in the Next Decade (2019–28) to Be Ranked Among the Top 10
Warmest Years Globally?" *Bulletin of the American Meteorological
Society* 101, no. 5 (May 2020): 655–663.

43 Florian Reber, "Tales of Change," Earth, September 9, 2019, https://
www.talesofchange.earth/post/i-have-been-a-firefighter-for-30-years-
what-i-see-now-scares-me

44 Christina Anderson and Alan Cowell, "Heat Wave Scorches Sweden
as Wildfires Rage in the Arctic Circle," *The New York Times*, July 19,
2018.

45 Sean McAllister, "There Could Be 1.2 Billion Climate Refugees
by 2050. Here's What You Need to Know," *Zurich Magazine*,
September 19, 2023, https://www.zurich.com/media/magazine/2022/
there-could-be-1-2-billion-climate-refugees-by-2050-here-s-what-
you-need-to-know

46 Graham Readfearn and Adam Morton, "Almost 3 Billion Animals Affected by Australia's Bushfires, Report Shows," *The Guardian*, July 28, 2020.

47 Linda Mearns, Lunch Conversation, June 2, 2020.

48 Ben Schiller, "After Years of Progress, Worldwide Hunger Is Once Again on the Rise," Fast Company, September 28, 2017, https://www.fastcompany.com/40469995/after-years-of-progress-worldwide-hunger-is-once-again-on-the-increase

49 "The State of Food Security and Nutrition in the World 2021," Food and Agriculture Organization of the United Nations, 2021, https://www.fao.org/interactive/state-of-food-security-nutrition/2021/en/

50 Martha Henriques, "Climate Change: The 1.5C Threshold Explained," BBC, February 8, 2024, https://www.bbc.com/future/article/20231130-climate-crisis-the-15c-global-warming-threshold-explained

51 "Prevalence of Undernourishment (% of Population)," World Bank Open Data, 2021, https://data.worldbank.org/indicator/SN.ITK.DEFC.ZS

52 "Food Security Data and Research," World Bank Group, May 31, 2024, https://www.worldbank.org/en/topic/agriculture/brief/food-security-update/data-and-research

53 Toby Ord, *The Precipice: Existential Risk and the Future of Humanity* (New York: Hachette Book Group, 2020), 103.

54 Toby Ord, *The Precipice: Existential Risk and the Future of Humanity* (New York: Hachette Book Group, 2020), 106.

55 Nick Bostrom and Milan M. Cirkovic, *Global Catastophic Risks* (Oxford: Oxford University Press, 2011).

56 Toby Ord, *The Precipice: Existential Risk and the Future of Humanity* (New York: Hachette Book Group, 2020), 6.

57 Toby Ord, *The Precipice: Existential Risk and the Future of Humanity* (New York: Hachette Book Group, 2020), 112.

58 Michael A, "Some Thoughts on Toby Ord's Existential Risk Estimates," April 6, 2020, https://forum.effectivealtruism.org/posts/Z5KZ2cui8WDjyF6gJ/some-thoughts-on-toby-ord-s-existential-risk-estimates

59 Eva Kappas, "The Fossil Fuel Lobbyist's New Groove," Climate and Capital Media, August 1, 2023, https://www.climateandcapitalmedia.com/the-fossil-fuel-lobbyists-new-groove/

60 Eva Kappas, "The Fossil Fuel Lobbyist's New Groove," Climate and Capital Media, August 1, 2023, https://www.climateandcapitalmedia.com/the-fossil-fuel-lobbyists-new-groove/

61 Future of Life Institute. "Future of Life Award," June 7, 2022, https://futureoflife.org/project/future-of-life-award/

62 David Krieger, "Nuclear Weapons: New Modes of Thinking," Nuclear Age Peace Foundation, November 21, 2019, https://www.waging-peace.org/wp-content/uploads/2019/11/new_modes_of_thinking.pdf

63 Krystyna Marcinek, "Nuclear Weapons and Putin's 'Holy War,'" The Hill, November 1, 2022, https://thehill.com/opinion/national-security/3714387-nuclear-weapons-and-putins-holy-war/

64 Nick Bostrom, "The Vulnerable World Hypothesis," Global Policy 10, no. 4 (September 6, 2019): 455–476.

65 Andrew Marshall, "It Gassed the Tokyo Subway, Microwaved Its Enemies and Tortured Its Members. So Why Is the Aum Cult Thriving?" The Guardian, July 15, 1999.

66 David Lambert and Sam Hill, "Thank You Dr. Fauci," Newsweek, April 15, 2020, https://www.newsweek.com/thank-you-dr-fauci-public-health-1498110

67 Toby Ord, The Precipice: Existential Risk and the Future of Humanity (New York: Hachette Book Group, 2020), 126.

68 R. Daniel Bressler and Chris Bakerlee, "'Designer Bugs': How the Next Pandemic Might Come From a Lab," Vox, December 6, 2018, https://www.vox.com/future-perfect/2018/12/6/18127430/superbugs-biotech-pathogens-biorisk-pandemic

69 Toby Ord, The Precipice: Existential Risk and the Future of Humanity (New York: Hachette Book Group, 2020), 57.

70 Toby Ord, The Precipice: Existential Risk and the Future of Humanity (New York: Hachette Book Group, 2020), 168.

71 Tim Urban, "The Artificial Intelligence Revolution: Part 1," Wait But Why (blog), January 22, 2015, https://waitbutwhy.com/2015/01/artificial-intelligence-revolution-1.html

72 Neil Docherty and David Fanning, "In the Age of AI," Frontline, 2019, https://www.pbs.org/wgbh/frontline/documentary/in-the-age-of-ai/transcript/

73 Steven Pinker, "AI Won't Takeover the World, and What Our Fears of the Robopocalypse Reveal," Big Think, August 10, 2016, https://bigthink.com/videos/steven-pinker-on-artificial-intelligence-apocalypse/

74 Peter Singer, The Expanding Circle (New York: Farrar, Straus and Giroux, 1981).

75 https://www.threads.net/@voxdotcom/post/C011UQWA4U5

76 James Felton, "How an AI Asked to Produce Paperclips Could End Up Destroying Humanity," IFLScience, April 13, 2023, https://www.

iflscience.com/how-an-ai-asked-to-produce-paperclips-could-end-up-wiping-out-humanity-68432

77 Toby Ord, *The Precipice: Existential Risk and the Future of Humanity* (New York: Hachette Book Group, 2020), 143.

78 Dan Hendrycks, "The Darwinian Argument for Worrying About AI," *Time*, May 31, 2023, https://time.com/6283958/darwinian-argument-for-worrying-about-ai/

79 Dan Hendrycks, "Natural Selection Favors AIs Over Humans," arXiv.org, March 2023, https://arxiv.org/abs/2303.16200

80 https://www.threads.net/@voxdotcom/post/C011UQWA4U5

81 Li Cohen, "Animal Populations Have Plummeted by Nearly 70% in Last 50 Years, New Report Says," CBS News, October 14, 2022, https://www.cbsnews.com/news/animal-populations-plummeted-by-nearly-70-percent-last-50-years-new-report/

82 Global Alliance for the Rights of Nature (GARN), Cochabamba, Bolivia, April 22, 2010, https://www.garn.org/universal-declaration-for-the-rights-of-mother-earth/

83 Brian Trelstad, Nien-hê Hsieh, Michael Norris, and Susan Pinckney, "Patagonia: 'Earth Is Now Our Only Shareholder' – Case – Faculty & Research," Harvard Business School, revised September 2023, https://www.hbs.edu/faculty/Pages/item.aspx?num=63834

84 Cy Wakeman, "Confidence Vs. Ego: The Difference Between Success and Self-Sabotage," *Forbes*, November 23.

85 Paul Polman and Andrew Winston, *Net Positive* (Brighton, MA: Harvard Business Review Press, 2021).

86 Geoffrey James, "Why Unilever Stopped Issuing Quarterly Reports," *Inc.*, January 23, 2018, https://www.inc.com/geoffrey-james/why-unilever-stopped-issuing-quarterly-reports.html

87 Paul Hawken, Amory Lovins, and L. Hunter Lovins, *Natural Capitalism* (New York: Routledge, 2000).

88 L. Hunter Lovins, Stewart Wallis, Anders Wijkman, and John Fullerton, *A Finer Future* (Canada: New Society Publishers, 2018).

89 Jim Harter, "3 Key Insights into the Global Workplace," June 12, 2024, https://www.gallup.com/workplace/645416/key-insights-global-workplace.aspx

90 Geoffrey James, "Why Unilever Stopped Issuing Quarterly Reports," *Inc.*, January 23, 2018, https://www.inc.com/geoffrey-james/why-unilever-stopped-issuing-quarterly-reports.html

91 Simon Sinek, *Start With Why: How Great Leaders Inspire Everyone to Take Action* (Penguin Books, 2009).

92 Zameena Mejia, "Nearly 9 out of 10 Millennials Would Consider Taking a Pay Cut to Get This," CNBC, June 28, 2018, https://www.cnbc.com/2018/06/27/nearly-9-out-of-10-millennials-would-consider-a-pay-cut-to-get-this.html

93 Patrick Bolton and Marcin Kacperczyk, "Do Investors Care About Carbon Risk?" *Journal of Financial Economics* 142, no 2 (2021): 517–549.

94 Andrew Winston, *The Big Pivot* (Brighton, MA: Harvard Business Review Press, 2014).

95 Paul Polman and Andrew Winston, *Net Positive* (Brighton, MA: Harvard Business Review Press, 2021).

96 Jerry D. Belloit, "The All-Electric Vehicle: Is It Time?" In 41st Annual Meeting of the Northeastern Association of Business, Economics and Technology, November 2018, 8–17.

97 Brad Plumer and Lisa Friedman, "A Swaggering Clean Energy Pioneer, with $400 Billion to Hand Out," *The New York Times*, May 11, 2023, https://www.nytimes.com/2023/05/11/climate/jigar-shah-climate-biden.html

98 "Does Fear Motivate Workers—or Make Things Worse?" Knowledge at Wharton, December 4, 2018, https://knowledge.wharton.upenn.edu/podcast/knowledge-at-wharton-podcast/fear-motivate-workers-make-things-worse/#:~:text=In%20some%20circles%2C%20the%20conventional,especially%20when%20creativity%20is%20necessary.

99 "Does Fear Motivate Workers—or Make Things Worse?" Knowledge at Wharton, December 4, 2018, https://knowledge.wharton.upenn.edu/podcast/knowledge-at-wharton-podcast/fear-motivate-workers-make-things-worse/#:~:text=In%20some%20circles%2C%20the%20conventional,especially%20when%20creativity%20is%20necessary.

100 Amy C. Edmondson, "Learning From Mistakes Is Easier Said Than Done: Group and Organizational Influences on the Detection and Correction of Human Error," *The Journal of Applied Behavioral Science* 32, no 1 (1996): 5–28.

101 Will Kenton, "Power-Distance Index (PDI): Definition: How It Works, and Examples," *Investopedia*, updated January 07, 2024, https://www.investopedia.com/terms/p/power-distance-index-pdi.asp

102 Malcolm Gladwell, *Outliers: The Story of Success* (Little, Brown and Company, 2008).

103 Chip Bell, "Reviving the Lost Art of Forgiveness," *Forbes*, June 16, 2022, https://www.forbes.com/sites/chipbell/2022/06/15/reviving-the-lost-art-of-forgiveness/#

104 John Bettersby, "Mandela to Factions: Throw Guns into Sea," *The Christian Science Monitor*, February 26, 1990, https://www.csmonitor.com/1990/0226/o1john.html

105 https://www.brainyquote.com/quotes/idi_amin_556179

106 David F. Larcker, Charles A. O'Reilly, Brian Tayan, and Anastasia A. Zakolyukina, "Are Narcissistic CEOs All That Bad?" *Rock Center for Corporate Governance at Stanford University Working Paper*, October 2021.

107 Cy Wakeman, "Confidence Vs. Ego: The Difference Between Success and Self-Sabotage," *Forbes*, November 23, 2015.

108 Mark Murray Todd, Domenico Montanaro, NBC's Chuck, and Brooke Brower, "Does Obama Think Steve Jobs Didn't Build Apple?" NBC News, July 18, 2012, https://www.nbcnews.com/news/world/does-obama-think-steve-jobs-didnt-build-apple-flna893766

109 Andy Bailey, "The Self-Made Myth: All Business Leaders Had Help Along the Way," *Forbes*, December 18, 2018.

110 Victor Lipman, "66% of Employees Would Quit if They Feel Unappreciated," *Forbes*, updated June 25, 2018.

111 Andy Bailey, "The Self-Made Myth: All Business Leaders Had Help Along the Way," *Forbes*, December 18, 2018.

112 Chelsea Conaboy, "Maternal Instinct Is a Myth That Men Created," *The New York Times*, August 26, 2023.

113 Barry S. Hewlett and Steve Winn, "Allomaternal Nursing in Humans," *Current Anthropology 55*, no 2 (2014): 200–229.

114 Teresa Salhi, "Feminine and Masculine Wound Traits – Improving Your Relationships," *Empower The Dream*, April 30, 2020, https://empowerthedream.com/feminine-and-masculine-wound-traits-improving-your-relationships/

115 Heryna Oktaviana Kurniawati, "Gender Issues Towards Communication Aspects on Women Leadership Styles in Construction Company," In *6th International Conference on Social and Political Sciences* (2020), 82–88, Atlantis Press, 2020.

116 Marvin E. Wolfgang, *Patterns in Criminal Homicide* (University of Pennsylvania Press, 2016).

117 "Myth & Facts," Hope of East Central Illinois, accessed August 11, 2024, https://hope-eci.org/myth-facts/

118 Barack Obama, "President Barack Obama Says, 'This Is What a Feminist Looks Like,'" *Glamour*, August 4, 2016, https://www.glamour.com/story/glamour-exclusive-president-barack-obama-says-this-is-what-a-feminist-looks-like

119 Susan R. Fisk and Jon Overton, "Bold or Reckless? The Impact of Workplace Risk-Taking on Attributions and Expected Outcomes," *Plos One* 15, no 3 (2020).

120 Eleanor Roosevelt, Quote, https://www.goodreads.com/quotes/25106-do-one-thing-every-day-that-scares-you

121 Rolf Dobelli, *The Art of Thinking Clearly: The Secrets of Perfect Decision-Making* (Hachette, 2013).

122 Jonathan Haidt, *The Righteous Mind: Why Good People Are Divided by Politics and Religion* (New York: Knopf Doubleday Publishing Group, 2012).

123 Abigail Geiger, "Political Polarization in the American Public," Pew Research Center, June 12, 2014, https://www.pewresearch.org/politics/2014/06/12/political-polarization-in-the-american-public/

124 Jonathan Haidt, *The Righteous Mind: Why Good People Are Divided by Politics and Religion* (New York: Knopf Doubleday Publishing Group, 2012).

125 James Clear, *Atomic Habits: An Easy & Proven Way to Build Good Habits & Break Bad Ones* (Penguin, 2018).

126 Nathan Robinson, "The 'Ted Cruz is Smart' Trap: Why This Garbage Is False – and Dangerous," July 28, 2014, https://www.salon.com/2014/07/28/the_ted_cruz_is_smart_trap_why_this_garbage_is_false_and_dangerous/

127 Rolf Dobelli, *The Art of Thinking Clearly: The Secrets of Perfect Decision-Making* (Hachette, 2013).

128 Paul Lewis, Seán Clarke, Caelainn Barr, Niko Kommenda, and Josh Holder, "Revealed: One in Four Europeans Vote Populist," *The Guardian*, November 20, 2018, https://www.theguardian.com/world/ng-interactive/2018/nov/20/revealed-one-in-four-europeans-vote-populist

129 https://dictionary.cambridge.org/us/dictionary/english/populism

130 https://en.wikipedia.org/wiki/Populism

131 Ravishankar, "Tim Urban's 1,000-Page Book on Human History," *Story Rules*, April 22, 2023, https://www.storyrules.com/chatgpt-is-a-photocopier-2/

132 Rose McDermott and Peter K. Hatemi, "To Go Forward, We Must Look Back: The Importance of Evolutionary Psychology for

Understanding Modern Politics," *Evolutionary Psychology* 16, no 2 (2018).

133 Steven Pinker, "Violence Vanquished," *The Wall Street Journal*, September 24, 2011.

134 Rose McDermott and Peter K. Hatemi, "To Go Forward, We Must Look Back: The Importance of Evolutionary Psychology for Understanding Modern Politics," *Evolutionary Psychology* 16, no 2 (2018).

135 Kate Whiting and HyoJin Park, "This is why 'polycrisis' is a useful way of looking at the world right now," World Economic forum, Mar 7, 2023, https://www.weforum.org/stories/2023/03/polycrisis-adam-tooze-historian-explains/#:~:text="If%20you've%20been%20feeling,his%20interview%20for%20Radio%20Davos.

136 Leo Tolstoy, *War and Peace* (Random House, 2015), 8.

137 Toby Ord, *The Precipice: Existential Risk and the Future of Humanity* (New York: Hachette Book Group, 2020), 4.

138 Ray Kurzweil, "The Law of Accelerating Returns." In: Teuscher, C. (ed.) *Alan Turing: Life and Legacy of a Great Thinker* (Berlin, Heidelberg: Springer-Verlag), 381–416.

139 Tim Urban, "The Artificial Intelligence Revolution: Part 1," Wait But Why (blog), January 22, 2015, https://waitbutwhy.com/2015/01/artificial-intelligence-revolution-1.html

140 Richard Hofstadter, *Anti-Intellectualism in American Life* (Vintage, 2012).

141 "A Quote by George R.R. Martin," accessed August 12, 2024, https://www.goodreads.com/quotes/9284815-the-battle-between-good-and-evil-is-a-legitimate-theme

142 Ava Kalinauskas and Samuel Garrett, "'I Don't Really Care What Happens to Ukraine': What a JD Vance Vice Presidency Could Mean for the World," Conversation, July 16, 2024, https://theconversation.com/i-dont-really-care-what-happens-to-ukraine-what-a-jd-vance-vice-presidency-could-mean-for-the-world-234815

143 Anthony Zurcher, "Trump Echoes Russia as He Upends US Position on Ukraine," BBC News, February 19, 2025.

144 Noga Levy-Rapoport, "Isolationism Is Deadly. Only Global Collective Action Can Save Us," *The Guardian*, March 15, 2019, https://www.theguardian.com/commentisfree/2019/mar/15/isolationism-climate-change-global-collective-action

145 "Elizabeth Holmes," *Forbes Profile*, Forbes, accessed August 12, 2024, https://www.forbes.com/profile/elizabeth-holmes/

146 Vivia Chen, "Why Women Feel Relief That Elizabeth Holmes Got Convicted," *Bloomberg Law*, January 10, 2022, https://news. bloomberglaw.com/us-law-week/why-women-feel-relief-that-elizabeth-holmes-got-convicted

147 Ellen Pao, "Opinion: The Elizabeth Holmes Trial Is a Wake-Up Call for Sexism in Tech," *The New York Times*, September 16, 2021, https://www.nytimes.com/2021/09/15/opinion/elizabeth-holmes-trial-sexism.html

148 Lara Stemple, "Elizabeth Holmes' Conviction Is Actually a Win for Women," *Slate*, January 4, 2022, https://slate.com/news-and-politics/ 2022/01/guilty-verdict-in-elizabeth-holmes-trial-is-a-win-for-women. html

149 Alice Evans, "Ten Thousand Years of Patriarchy!" *Alice Evans* (Alice Evans, December 24, 2021), https://www.ggd.world/p/ten-thousand-years-of-patriarchy-1

150 https://www.the-independent.com/news/world/asia/dalai-lama-women-attractive-successor-female-not-much-use-a8984356.html

151 Laura Clancy and Sarah Austin, "About a Third of UN Member States Have Ever Had a Woman Leader," Pew Research Center, March 28, 2023, https://www.pewresearch.org/short-reads/2023/03/28/women-leaders-around-the-world/

152 Linda Robinson and Noel James, "Women's Power Index," Council on Foreign Relations, last updated March 14, 2024, https://www. cfr.org/article/womens-power-index

153 Paul Taylor, "Men or Women: Who's the Better Leader?" Pew Research Center, August 25, 2008, https://www.pewresearch.org/ wp-content/uploads/sites/3/2010/10/gender-leadership.pdf

154 Paul Taylor, "Men Or Women: Who's the Better Leader?" Pew Research Center, August 25, 2008, https://www.pewresearch.org/ wp-content/uploads/sites/3/2010/10/gender-leadership.pdf

155 World Economic Forum, "104 countries have laws that prevent women from working in some jobs," August 13, 2018, https:// www.weforum.org/stories/2018/08/104-countries-have-laws-that-prevent-women-from-working-in-some-jobs/

156 Susan Chira, "Why Women Aren't C.E.O.s, According to Women Who Almost Were," *The New York Times*, July 21, 2017.

157 Mwanza, Kevin, "Less Than Two Percent of Land in Kenya Issued to Women Despite Legal Gains," *Reuters*, March 13, 2018, https:// www.reuters.com/article/world/less-than-two-percent-of-land-in-kenya-issued-to-women-despite-legal-gains-idUSKCN1GP22A/

158 John Ross, Karen Hardee, Rebecca Rosenberg, and Imelda Zosa-Feranil, "Inequities in Family Planning in Low- and Middle-Income Countries," *Global Health, Science and Practice* 11, no 3, June 21, 2023.

159 Action Education, "773 million people worldwide would not be able to read this article," September 8, 2023, https://action-education.org/en/773-million-people-not-read-this-article/

160 UNESCO, "Afghanistan: 1.4 million girls still banned from school by de facto authorities," August 15, 2024, https://www.unesco.org/en/articles/afghanistan-14-million-girls-still-banned-school-de-facto-authorities

161 Paul Hawken, *Drawdown: The Most Comprehensive Plan Ever Proposed to Reverse Global Warming* (Penguin, 2017).

162 Guttmacher, "State Laws and Policies", Mar 26, 2025, https://www.guttmacher.org/state-policy/explore/state-policies-abortion-bans#:~:text=shortly%20after%20birth.-,Highlights,bans%20based%20on%20gestational%20duration.

163 "Public Opinion on Abortion," Pew Research Center, May 13, 2024, https://www.pewresearch.org/religion/fact-sheet/public-opinion-on-abortion/

164 https://lbcommuter.com/police-accountability/

165 Richard C. Lewis, "A Heart that Beats (Almost) Like Our Own," *Iowa Now*, Oct 22, 2021, https://now.uiowa.edu/news/2021/10/heart-beats-almost-our-own

166 https://en.wikipedia.org/wiki/List_of_animals_by_number_of_neurons

167 World Health Organization, "Child Mortality (Under 5 Years)," January 28, 2022, https://www.who.int/news-room/fact-sheets/detail/levels-and-trends-in-child-under-5-mortality-in-2020

168 Susan Chira, "Why Women Aren't C.E.O.s, According to Women Who Almost Were," *The New York Times*, July 21, 2017.

169 Eden King and Kristen Jones, "Why Subtle Bias Is So Often Worse Than Blatant Discrimination," *Harvard Business Review* 94, no 7–8 (2016): 34–40.

170 Eliza Anyangwe and Melissa Mahtami, "What Is Patriarchy? What Does it Mean and Why Is Everyone Talking About It?" CNN, 2003, https://www.cnn.com/2023/08/03/world/what-is-patriarchy-explainer-as-equals-intl-cmd/index.html#:~:text=Is%20the%20US%20a%20patriarchy,recent%20efforts%20to%20revive%20it.

171 "Gender Pay Gap in U.S Hasn't Changed Much in Two decades," Pew Research Center, March 1, 2023, https://www.pewresearch.org/short-reads/2023/03/01/gender-pay-gap-facts/

172 Lyta Gold, "Evolutionary Psychology Quiz," *Current Affairs*, May 5, 2019, https://www.currentaffairs.org/news/2019/05/evolutionary-psychology-quiz

173 Kate Plummer, "11 of Marine Le Pen's Most Controversial Quotes," *Indy100*, April 23, 2022, https://www.indy100.com/politics/marine-le-pen-quotes-france

174 Justin Winters and Lindsey Jean Schueman, "Why Women Are Key to Solving the Climate Crisis," *One Earth*, June 5, 2024, https://www.oneearth.org/why-women-are-key-to-solving-the-climate-crisis/

175 Jon Henley, "Female-Led Countries Handled Coronavirus Better, Study Suggests," *The Guardian*, August 18, 2020, https://www.theguardian.com/world/2020/aug/18/female-led-countries-handled-coronavirus-better-study-jacinda-ardern-angela-merkel

176 Susanne Bruckmüller and Nyla R. Branscombe, "How Women End Up on the 'Glass Cliff,'" *Harvard Business Review* 89, no 1–2 (2011): 26–26.

177 Lynnette C. Zelezny, Poh-Pheng Chua, and Christina Aldrich, "New Ways of Thinking About Environmentalism: Elaborating on Gender Differences in Environmentalism," *Journal of Social Issues* 56, no 3 (2000): 443–457.

178 World Economic Forum, "Women grow 70% of Africa's food. But have few rights over the land they tend," March 21, 2018, https://www.weforum.org/stories/2018/03/women-farmers-food-production-land-rights/#:~:text=Studies%20show%20that%20women%20account,their%20land%20and%20property%20rights

179 *Empowering Women Farmers to End Hunger and Poverty*, Oxfam International, May 25, 2022, https://www.oxfam.org/en/empowering-women-farmers-end-hunger-and-poverty

180 Interview, Hunter Lovins, November 20, 2021.

181 Justin Winters and Lindsey Jean Schueman, "Why Women Are Key to Solving the Climate Crisis," *One Earth*, June 5, 2024, https://www.oneearth.org/why-women-are-key-to-solving-the-climate-crisis/

182 https://en.wikipedia.org/wiki/Nemonte_Nenquimo

183 Justin Winters and Lindsey Jean Schueman, "Why Women Are Key to Solving the Climate Crisis," *One Earth*, June 5, 2024, https://www.oneearth.org/why-women-are-key-to-solving-the-climate-crisis/

184 Greta Thunberg, "'You Did Not Act in Time': Greta Thunberg's Full Speech to MPs," *The Guardian*, April 23, 2019.

185 Greta Thunberg, "'You Did Not Act in Time': Greta Thunberg's Full Speech to MPs," *The Guardian*, April 23, 2019.

186 Veronica Stracqualursi, "Trump Mocks Teenage Climate Activist Greta Thunberg," *CNN*, September 24, 2019, https://edition.cnn.com/2019/09/24/politics/trump-greta-thunberg-climate-change-trnd/index.html

187 Lynnette C. Zelezny, Poh-Pheng Chua, and Christina Aldrich, "New Ways of Thinking About Environmentalism: Elaborating on Gender Differences in Environmentalism," *Journal of Social Issues* 56, no 3 (2000): 443–457.

188 Climate Action, "Global Landscapes Forum, March 7, 2021," https://www.globallandscapesforum.org/glf-news/meet-16-women-leading-earths-restoration-as-the-world-enters-last-decade-for-climate-action/

189 Hani Zainulbhai, "Women, More Than Men, Say Climate Change Will Harm Them Personally," Pew Research Center, December 2, 2015, https://www.pewresearch.org/short-reads/2015/12/02/women-more-than-men-say-climate-change-will-harm-them-personally/

190 "The Dangers of Gender Inequality in Health Care," Surest (blog), Surest, August 18, 2021, https://www.surest.com/blog/dangers-of-gender-inequality-in-health-care

191 Lynnette C. Zelezny, Poh-Pheng Chua, and Christina Aldrich, "New Ways of Thinking About Environmentalism: Elaborating on Gender Differences in Environmentalism," *Journal of Social Issues* 56, no. 3 (2000): 443–457.

192 Zainab Waheed, "Climate Change's Greatest Victims Are Women and Girls," UNICEF South Asia, December 8, 2023, https://www.unicef.org/rosa/blog/climate-changes-greatest-victims-are-women-and-girls

193 "Explainer: How Gender Inequality and Climate Change Are Interconnected," UN Women, February 28, 2022, https://www.unwomen.org/en/news-stories/explainer/2022/02/explainer-how-gender-inequality-and-climate-change-are-interconnected

194 Justin Winters and Lindsey Jean Schueman, "Why Women Are Key to Solving the Climate Crisis," *One Earth*, June 5, 2024, https://www.oneearth.org/why-women-are-key-to-solving-the-climate-crisis/

195 Duncan Thomas, "Intra-Household Resource Allocation: An Inferential Approach," *Journal of Human Resources* 25, no. 4 (Autumn 1990): 635–664.

196 Judith Bruce, and Cynthia B. Lloyd, "Finding the Ties That Bind: Beyond Headship and Household," in Lawrence Haddad, John

Hoddinott, and Harald Alderman (Eds), *Intrahousehold Resources Allocation in Developing Countries, Methods, Models, and Policy* (Baltimore, MD: International Food Policy Research Institute and Johns Hopkins University Press, 1997).

197 Daniel J. Sandberg, "When Women Lead, Firms Win," SP Global, October 16, 2019.

198 "The Power of Parity: How Advancing Women's Equality Can Add $12 Trillion to Global Growth," *McKinsey Global Institute*, September 1, 2015, https://www.mckinsey.com/featured-insights/employment-and-growth/how-advancing-womens-equality-can-add-12-trillion-to-global-growth

199 Christina Kwauk, "Why Captain Planet Should Have Been a Woman," *Brookings*, March 28, 2019, https://www.brookings.edu/articles/why-captain-planet-should-have-been-a-woman/

200 "Handbook on Promoting Women's Participation in Political Parties," OSCE, July 7, 2014, https://www.osce.org/files/f/documents/e/f/120877.pdf

201 Ian Johnston, "Humans Evolved to Have an Instinct for Deadly Violence, Researchers Find," *The Independent*, September 28, 2016, https://www.independent.co.uk/news/science/human-evolution-violence-instinct-to-kill-murder-each-other-a7335491.html

202 "Women, Conflict and Peacebuilding," Commission for Victims and Survivors, March 8, 2023, https://www.cvsni.org/news/women-conflict-and-peacebuilding/

203 "Tackling Liberia's High Rape Rate," UNHCR, July 18, 2014, https://webarchive.archive.unhcr.org/20230521055240/https://www.refworld.org/docid/53cfa1e94.html

204 "Resisting Violence-Kathleen B. Jones," Amor Mundi, Hannah Arendt Center for Politics and Humanities at Bard College, November 11, 2011, https://hac.bard.edu/amor-mundi/resisting-violence-kathleen-b-jones-2011-11-21

205 "President Ellen Johnson Sirleaf," Mo Ibrahim Foundation, 2017, https://mo.ibrahim.foundation/prize/laureates/ellen-johnson-sirleaf

206 Michael Stankosky and Carolyn R. Baldanza, *21 for 21: Leading the 21st Century Global Enterprise* (Emerald Publishing Limited, 2018), 17–27.

207 "Mentoring: The Missing Link to Small Business Growth and Survival," SBA (blog), U.S. Small Business Administration, February 4, 2019, https://www.sba.gov/blog/mentoring-missing-link-small-business-growth-survival

208 "Women in the Workplace 2016," *McKinsey & Company*, April 1, 2017, https://edge.berkeley.edu/wp-content/uploads/2017/08/Women-in-the-Workplace-2016-1.pdf

209 Max Roser, "Access to Basic Education: Almost 60 Million Children of Primary School Age Are Not in School," November 2, 2021, https://ourworldindata.org/children-not-in-school

210 TIME Magazine, "Top 10 Bushisms" [stump speech in Florence, South Carolina on January 11, 2000] https://content.time.com/time/specials/packages/article/0,28804,1870938_1870943_1870949,00.html

211 https://en.wikipedia.org/wiki/Maria_Montessori

212 Mike Colagrossi, "10 Reasons Why Finland's Education System Is the Best in the World," *Big Think*, September 9, 2018, https://bigthink.com/the-present/finland-education-system-2/

213 Stephen J. Dubner (Host). (2012, October 11). The Cobra Effect [Podcast]. *Freakonomics*, episode 96. https://freakonomics.com/podcast/the-cobra-effect-2/

214 Pasi Sahlberg, *Finnish Lessons 2.0: What Can the World Learn from Educational Change in Finland?* (New York: Teachers College Press, 2015).

215 Pasi Sahlberg, "Rethinking Accountability in a Knowledge Society," *Journal of Educational Change* 11, no. 1 (2010): 45–61.

216 Mike Colagrossi, "10 Reasons Why Finland's Education System Is the Best in the World," *Big Think*, September 9, 2018, https://bigthink.com/the-present/finland-education-system-2/

217 Christophe Vandenberghe, "Erasmus International – 10 Reasons Why Finland's Education System Is the Best in the World," *Erasmus International*, February 27, 2021, https://www.erasmus.international/10-reasons-why-finlands-education-system-is-the-best-in-the-world/

218 Malcolm Gladwell, *Outliers: The Story of Success* (Little, Brown and Company, 2008).

219 Erasmus International, "10 Reasons Why Finland's Education System Is the Best in the World," https://www.erasmus.international/10-reasons-why-finlands-education-system-is-the-best-in-the-world/#:~:text=While%20most%20Americans%20and%20other,Real%20winners%20do%20not%20compete

220 MorningFUTURE, "Empathy? In Denmark, They're Learning It in School," September 1, 2020, https://thedanishway.com/empathy-in-denmark-theyre-learning-it-in-school/

221 Försäkringskassan, "Parental benefits", Nov 18, 2024, https://www.forsakringskassan.se/english/parents/when-the-child-is-born/parental-benefit

222 Jennifer Liu, "The Typical CEO Makes Nearly 200 Times More Than Their Workers," *CNBC*, Jun 5, 2024, https://www.cnbc.com/2024/06/05/typical-ceo-makes-nearly-200-times-more-than-their-workers.html

223 "Global Education Monitoring Report," United Nations Educational, Scientific and Cultural Organization, 2023.

224 Tom Rath and Barry Conchie, *Strengths Based Leadership: Great Leaders, Teams, and Why People Follow* (Gallup Press, 2009).

225 "Getting the Right People in the Right Seats Over Time," Jim Collins – Video/Audio, accessed August 14, 2024, https://www.jim-collins.com/media_topics/inTheRightSeats.html

226 Simon Kuznets, "National Income and Industrial Structure," *Econometrica: Journal of the Econometric Society* (1949): 205–241.

227 Luca Di Leo, "Oil Spill May End Up Lifting GDP Slightly," *The Wall Street Journal*, June 15, 2010, https://www.wsj.com/articles/BL-REB-10524

228 R. Strand, Z. Kovacic, S. Funtowicz, L. Benini, and A. Jesus, "Growth Without Economic Growth," *European Environment Agency*, Briefing no. 28 (2020), January 13, 2021, https://www.eea.europa.eu/publications/growth-without-economic-growth

229 Simon Kuznets, "National Income and Industrial Structure," *Econometrica: Journal of the Econometric Society* (1949): 205–241.

230 Inemesit Ukpanah, "Is Deforestation Bad for the Environment? Stats, Trends, and Facts," greenmatch.co.uk., last updated April 25, 2024, https://www.greenmatch.co.uk/blog/environmental-impact-of-deforestation

231 R. Strand, Z. Kovacic, S. Funtowicz, L. Benini, and A. Jesus, "Growth Without Economic Growth," *European Environment Agency*, Briefing no. 28 (2020), January 13, 2021, https://www.eea.europa.eu/publications/growth-without-economic-growth

232 Dave Ramsey, *The Total Money Makeover: Classic Edition: A Proven Plan for Financial Fitness* (Thomas Nelson, 2013), 31.

233 Kate Raworth, Interview by Nathan Robinson, *Current Affairs*, June 10, 2022, https://www.currentaffairs.org/news/2022/06/rethinking-endless-growth-with-doughnut-economics

234 Steven D. Levitt and Stephen J. Dubner, *SuperFreakonomics: Global Cooling, Patriotic Prostitutes, and Why Suicide Bombers Should Buy Life Insurance* (New York: William Morrow, 2009).

235 Jason Hickel, *Less is More: How Degrowth Will Save the World* (Random House, 2020).

236 Enrique Rivera, "William Shatner Experienced Profound Grief in Space. It Was the 'Overview Effect,'" *NPR*, October 23, 2022, https://www.npr.org/2022/10/23/1130482740/william-shatner-jeff-bezos-space-travel-overview-effect

237 "Time Left to the End of Seafood," *The World Counts*, accessed August 14, 2024, https://www.theworldcounts.com/challenges/planet-earth/oceans/overfishing-statistics

238 "Resources & Consumption," *Population Matters*, October 19, 2018, https://populationmatters.org/the-facts-resources-consumption/

239 "SDG Indicators," *Statistics Division, United Nations Statistics*, accessed August 14, 2024, https://unstats.un.org/sdgs/report/2019/goal-12/

240 Piya Sachdeva, "Should Investors Consider Happiness Rather Than GDP?" *Schroders*, September 1, 2021, https://www.schroders.com/en-ch/ch/professional/insights/should-investors-consider-happiness-rather-than-gdp/

241 "GDP Per Capita (Current US$)," *World Bank*, July 2, 2023.

242 J. F. Helliwell, R. Layard, J. D. Sachs, L. B. Aknin, J. E. De Neve, S. Wang, "World Happiness Report 2023 (11th ed.)," *Sustainable Development Solutions Network*, 2023.

243 Atul Gawande, "Costa Ricans Live Longer Than We Do. What's the Secret?" *The New Yorker*, August 23, 2021, https://www.newyorker.com/magazine/2021/08/30/costa-ricans-live-longer-than-we-do-whats-the-secret

244 "100% Renewable Energy in Costa Rica – Project Page," *World Future Council*, September 2, 2019, https://www.worldfuturecouncil.org/100-renewable-energy-costa-rica/

245 World Economic Forum, "Here Is Proof That Economic Wealth Does Not Guarantee the Best Quality of Life," July 4, 2016, https://www.weforum.org/stories/2016/07/here-is-proof-that-economic-wealth-does-not-guarantee-the-best-quality-of-life/#:~:text=%22The%20Social%20Progress%20Index%20proves,profit%20organisation%20Social%20Progress%20Imperative

246 Tomas Björkman, Jakob Trollbäck, Caroline Stiernstedt Sahlborn, Leif Edvinsson, and Mario de Vries, "Inner Development Goals – The Future Now Show," *Club of Amsterdam Journal*, August 22, 2022, https://clubofamsterdam.com/2022/08/22/inner-development-goals-the-future-now-show/

247 Tomas Björkman and Lene Andersen, *The Nordic Secret: A European Story of Beauty and Freedom*, Fri tanke, Sweden, November 7, 2017.

248 Caroline Criado Perez, *Invisible Women: Data Bias in a World Designed for Men* (New York: Abrams Press, 2019).

249 NBC News, "Unborn Babies Soaked in Chemicals, Study Finds," July 14, 2005, https://www.nbcnews.com/id/wbna8567514

250 "The Four Pillars of Gross National Happiness," Shivoy DMC, June 25, 2018, https://www.linkedin.com/pulse/four-pillars-gross-national-happiness-shivoy-dmc/

251 "The Macroeconomics of Happiness: A Case Study of Bhutan," *Berkeley Economic Review*, accessed August 14, 2024, https://econreview.studentorg.berkeley.edu/the-macroeconomics-of-happiness-a-case-study-of-bhutan/

252 "Poverty, Vulnerability and Welfare in Bhutan," *World Bank Group*, 2019, https://documents1.worldbank.org/curated/en/532991596197426851/pdf/Poverty-Vulnerability-and-Welfare-in-Bhutan-Progress-and-Challenges.pdf

253 "The Macroeconomics of Happiness: A Case Study of Bhutan," *Berkeley Economic Review*, August 14, 2024.

254 Annie Kelly, "Gross National Happiness in Bhutan: The Big Idea From a Tiny State That Could Change the World," *The Guardian*, December 1, 2012, https://www.theguardian.com/world/2012/dec/01/bhutan-wealth-happiness-counts

255 "Remarks at the University of Kansas, March 18, 1968," *John F. Kennedy Presidential Library and Museum*, accessed August 14, 2024, https://www.jfklibrary.org/learn/about-jfk/the-kennedy-family/robert-f-kennedy/robert-f-kennedy-speeches/remarks-at-the-university-of-kansas-march-18-1968

256 Ravishankar, "Tim Urban's 1,000-Page Book on Human History." *Story Rule*, April 22, 2023, https://www.storyrules.com/chatgpt-is-a-photocopier-2/

257 "The Persistence of QAnon in the Post-Trump Era: An Analysis of Who Believes the Conspiracies," *PRRI*, February 24, 2022, https://www.prri.org/research/the-persistence-of-qanon-in-the-post-trump-era-an-analysis-of-who-believes-the-conspiracies/

258 Yuval Noah Harari, "Yuval Noah Harari Extract: 'Humans Are a Post-Truth Species,'" *Guardian*, August 5, 2018.

259 Yuval Noah Harari, *21 Lessons for the 21st Century*, Random House, August 20, 2019

End Notes

260 "Putin's 'Surreal' Version of Ukrainian History Alarms Experts," *NBC News*, February 22, 2022, https://www.nbcnews.com/news/world/putin-russia-ukraine-history-speech-rcna17132

261 Dharna Noor, "Big oil spent $445 m in last election cycle to influence Trump and Congress," *Guardian*, Jan 23, 2025, https://www.theguardian.com/us-news/2025/jan/23/big-oil-445m-trump-congress

262 Victoria Masterson, World Economic Forum, July 5, 2021, https://www.weforum.org/stories/2021/07/renewables-cheapest-energy-source/

263 US. Senator Sheldon, Sen. Whitehouse on Fossil Fuel Subsidies, "We are Subsidizing the Danger," May 3, 2023, https://www.budget.senate.gov/chairman/newsroom/press/sen-whitehouse-on-fossil-fuel-subsidies-we-are-subsidizing-the-danger-

264 Geoff Dembicki, "Trump EPA Pick Lee Zeldin Backed by Texas Fracking Billionaire Tim Dunn," *DeSmog*, Nov 13, 2024, https://www.desmog.com/2024/11/13/trump-epa-pick-lee-zeldin-backed-by-texas-fracking-billionaire-tim-dunn/

265 US. Senator Sheldon, Sen. Whitehouse on Fossil Fuel Subsidies, "We are Subsidizing the Danger," May 3, 2023, https://www.budget.senate.gov/chairman/newsroom/press/sen-whitehouse-on-fossil-fuel-subsidies-we-are-subsidizing-the-danger-

266 U.S. Department of Energy, Job Creation and Economic Growth, 2023, https://www.energy.gov/eere/job-creation-and-economic-growth#:~:text=Jobs%20related%20to%20renewable%20energy,new%20electricity%20generation%20jobs%20in

267 U.S. Department of Energy, Job Creation and Economic Growth, 2023, https://www.energy.gov/eere/job-creation-and-economic-growth#:~:text=Jobs%20related%20to%20renewable%20energy,new%20electricity%20generation%20jobs%20i

268 Ed Yong, "Humans Unusually Murderous Mammals, Typically Murderous Primate," *Richard Dawkins Foundation*, October 4, 2016, https://richarddawkins.net/2016/10/humans-unusually-murderous-mammals-typically-murderous-primates/

269 https://en.wikipedia.org/wiki/Homicide_statistics_by_gender#:~:text=A%202013%20global%20study%20on,of%2010%20of%20the%20victims

270 https://en.wikipedia.org/wiki/World_War_II_casualties

271 UN Women, "Revisiting Rwanda Five Years After Record-Breaking Parliamentary Elections," August 13, 2018, https://www.unwomen.org/en/news/stories/2018/8/feature-rwanda-women-in-parliament

272 "Women's Participation in Peace Process," *Council of Foreign Relations*, https://www.cfr.org/womens-participation-in-peace-processes/

273 https://hsm.stackexchange.com/questions/7751/did-einstein-say-we-cannot-solve-our-problems-with-the-same-thinking-we-used-to

274 Sudanshu Palsule, Conversation with the Author and Other Participants During the United Nations University International Leadership Academy's meeting, "Leadership for Social Transition," in Amman, Jordan, July 2003. Mark Gerzon, *Leading Through Conflict* (Brighton, MA: Harvard Business Review Press, Chapter 7, p. 134, 2006).

275 Jeremy Lent, *The Web of Meaning: Integrating Science and Traditional Wisdom to Find our Place in the Universe* (Canada: New Society Publishers, 2022, Chapter 13, p. 364).

276 Toby Ord, *The Precipice: Existential Risk and the Future of Humanity* (New York: Hachette Book Group, 2020).

Appendix 1

Know Your Mindset

This book aims to challenge our ingrained mindset around leadership to one that I believe will serve us better for what is ahead. Mindsets control emotions and thinking, which in turn control our behaviors.

Do you know yours?

After reading this book, here are a few questions to start exploring your mindset.

- Based on their actions, have today's leaders prioritized humanity's well-being and our very survival?

- What masculine and feminine leadership traits do I lead with, are they harmonious and effective?

- What emotions guide my preference for certain leaders and where do they come from?

- What do I think would be the results if a full representation of humanity led humanity in businesses, religions, and nations?

- Do I know my core values, my purpose and what unique strengths I bring to this world and how I want to use them?

- How will my next purchase and consumption lead to well-being in my life?

- Which wolf do I feed?

Appendix 2

Know Yourself

As advised in my goal for this book "know thyself", and explored in Chapter 5 (From Classroom to Boardroom), we would all benefit greatly by coming life-long learners.

Do you know your core values, your purpose and what unique strengths you bring to this world and how to use them?

Please see below for a few helpful tools to get you started.

Your Strengths DNA

A great place to start is to learn more about your personal strengths and talents by taking Gallup's StrengthsFinder Assessment, which consists of 177 questions and takes about 45 minutes to complete. Only 1 in 30 million people will ever have the same Top 5 result, making it a highly personalized insight into your abilities. StrengthsFinder is used in about 90 percent of Fortune 500 businesses and, as of today, 30 million people have taken it worldwide. You can take the assessment as early as age 12, and we are slowly seeing the Strengths Movement starting to shape some K-12 schools and college campuses across the USA.

To find out more go to: http://www.gallup.com/cliftonstrengths

Your Core Values

Paramount to knowing your individual strengths is knowing your values. As we have touched on, we should continually reassess our values and ask ourselves if we place enough emphasis on what truly matters. Looking at our current situation, it is obvious that humanity has done a lot of good over the last few decades, but we are still in desperate need to go from good to great. There are a lot of wounds that still need healing if we are going to make it. One of my favorite assessments due to its simplicity, is Barrett's Value Assessment. There is one specific for individuals, if you are on the individual quest.

To find out more go to: https://www.valuescentre.com/tools-assessments/iva/

Your Unique Purpose

When we start exploring what gives us meaning in life, our purpose becomes quickly apparent. It is important to be pro-active about your purpose, life is short. Too often, we assume that one day we will have a grand epiphany that leads to us finding our true calling. But outside of Hollywood, this rarely happens. Instead of waiting for this life changing moment, answer these Zynergy Q12 simple questions to explore your feminine-nonlinear brain and start the journey of creating your purpose:

1. When do I feel the most alive?

2. What specifically am I engaged in?

3. Where am I?

4. With whom am I or am I by myself?

5. Why am I doing it?

6. How can I bring more of it into my life?

7. How would progress and success look like?

8. What is the next step?

9. Who will hold me accountable to take the next step?

10. By when will I take the next step?

11. Who/what do I honor in this process?

12. How do I celebrate the success of creating more purpose in my life?

Start Now!

What can I do today to make this day more meaningful?

If you like to discuss how you can bring the ideas presented in this book to your team, we would love to hear from you.

Please go to Zynergy International's website: http://zynergyinternational.com

Acknowledgments

This book wouldn't exist without the immense support I have received from family, friends, colleagues, and clients from around the world. While I often drew conclusions based on my own experiences and observations, I relied profoundly on the research and work done by many.

I'm forever grateful for the insights, wisdom and support from Roger Briggs, Barry Conchie, Doug Gardner, Mark Gerzon, Hunter Lovins, and Claudine Schneider. Doug Gardner connected me to David Lambert who helped me write this book, David, your talent and skillful research made my story come alive. Hunter Lovins, thank you for your incredible kindness and generosity editing this book, you took the time when you had no time.

Although I cannot acknowledge you all as you are in the hundreds, Hadeel Anabtawi, Chad Arnold, Melissa Arnold, Cynda Collins Arsenault, Gisèle Asplund, Pernilla Audibert, Tomas Björkman, Joan Blades, Mike Brady, David Bright, MD., Demitri Coupounas, Kim Coupounas, Sarah Dalton, Lisa Darrah, Amy Duckro, DO., Peggy Dulany, Goeff Elliott, Kate Elliott, Steve Fanning, Carol Frank, Martin Frick, PhD., Kent Gardner, Todd Goodrich, Jia Gottlieb, MD., AJ Grant, Katarina Greene, Catherine Greener, Bill Griffiths, Tamara Grivicic, Matt Harder, Joel Hartter, PhD., Christine Hibbard PhD., Wendy Hutt, Parker Johnson, Anneli Kansbod, Jesper Kansbod, Margo King, Kubs Lalchandani, Lara Latham, Louise Lindfors, Larry Linne, Brian Lisle, PhD., Pia Lisle MD., Julie Lockwood, Todd Lockwood, Becky Lyle, Alexander MacDonald, PhD., Susan MacDonald, Todd Minnis, John Moritz, Cassidy Murphy, Artem Nikulkov, Johanna Nilsson, TC North, PhD., Denise Pelusch, PhD., Aaron Perry, Richard Poley, Madeleine Pollak, Matt Query, Ingmar Rentzhog, Beau Rezendes, Abigail Schneider PhD.,

Dustin Simantob, Sina Simantob, Dan Smathers, Steve Smith, Howard Snooks, Bud Sorenson, Charlotte Sorenson, Linda Stankus, Ned Stankus, William Steding, PhD., John Steiner, Pamela Stewart, Maria Sunneborn, Oakleigh Thorne, PhD., Dalmas Tiampati, David Tusek, MD., Gisela Vaitaitis, Anders Wijkman, Maria Wik, George Wilson, Andrew Winston, Tommi Wolfe, Janet Woods, Jason Wykoff, Therese Wykoff, Ben Wyss, and Maria Wyss, your input, commitment, and support have greatly enriched my work, this book and my life.

I'm incredibly thankful to John Willig, my literary agent. John opened me up to the world of publishing and skillfully guided me every step on the way. John introduced me to Holly Bennion, my amazing editorial director at Hachette, imprint John Murray Business. John Willig and Holly Bennion saw what this book could be and the audience it could reach. A special thank you to the incredible team at Hachette, imprint John Murray Business, Meaghan Lim, Vivienne Church, Antonia Maxwell, Jen Campbell, Matt Young, Kaitlyn Shokes, and Melissa Carl. I'm honored to have been working with you.

Smith Publicity, you are the best, thank you to the entire team with a special gratitude to Marissa Eigenbrood, Corinne Moulder, Lauren Rosenthal, and Janet Shapiro.

I'm so grateful to my beloved parents Anna and Björn, and your forever-loving presence in my life, together with my rascal brothers Johan and Erik, who always make sure to keep me on my toes. Sending love and gratitude to my beautiful family Hubert, Alina, and Nicolas. We are all in this together, and I couldn't have done this without your love and support. Finally, an immense thank you, to all of you readers and followers out there. Only together can we change the leadership culture, our leaders, and our human and planetary trajectory. The best of humanity is yet to come, and with each one of you as a leader our future will be bright.

Edited by: Hunter Lovins
Graphical Design: Alina Belser-Brinck
Writing Place & Securus Locus, The Highland City Club, Boulder, Colorado

About the Author

MARIA BRINCK is the founder of the leadership advisory firm Zynergy International. She works with CEOs, board members, executives, business teams and HR professionals as a futurist and inspiring voice devoted to breaking up the traditional leadership monopoly.

Born and raised in Sweden and Algeria, Maria was educated in Sweden, France, and the USA, with a focus on international business. Her most transformative experience, reshaping her worldview, came when she lived and worked with the indigenous people in the Congo Basin Rainforest. It was in a remote part of Cameroon, while working on the rehabilitation of chimpanzees and gorillas, that she observed first-hand human planetary destruction and its consequences for all forms of life, but also the type of leadership we need to bring out the best in humanity.